Friends of the Lake District
the early years

by
John Cousins

Centre for North-West Regional Studies
Lancaster University
2009
Series Editor: Jean Turnbull

Friends of the Lake District: the early years

This volume is the 57th in a series of Occasional Papers published by the
Centre for North-West Regional Studies at the University of Lancaster

Text Copyright © John Cousins 2009

Designed, typeset, printed and bound by
4Word Ltd, Bristol

British Library Cataloguing in-Publication Data
A CIP catalogue entry for this book is available from the British Library

ISBN 978–1–86220–223–8

The publisher gratefully acknowledges a grant towards the cost of this publication
from the Friends of the Lake District

Contents

This book is dedicated to the memory of
Kenneth Spence (1887–1944)
and Henry Herbert Symonds (1885–1958)

List of Illustrations, Maps and Table

Illustrations

Maps

Table

Acknowledgements

At Friends of the Lake District (FLD) my thanks are due in particular to Ian Brodie and Jan Darrall for suggesting that an FLD history was long overdue, and encouraging and supporting me to undertake one: also special thanks to Andrew Forsyth for his continuing and more than full-hearted support once he had taken over the reins from Ian. FLD administrative staff have also been helpful, especially Cassie Nelson. I should also thank Mike Houston – FLD Secretary from 1976 until 1992. He gave his time willingly in several discussions we had about the early days of FLD, and also his time at the tiller; he also offered valuable and constructive comments on the early draft manuscript. Finally, at FLD, I should thank the President, Lord Judd, for agreeing to write a Foreword.

For providing me with interesting and invaluable information on aspects of the life of John Dower I should thank his son Professor Michael Dower; also James Cropper for sending me some useful background papers, and in particular the handwritten draft letter that his grandfather James Cropper, then Chairman of FLD, intended for, but never sent to, Sir Francis Acland (Forestry Commission member) during the 'afforestation quarrel' of 1934–1936.

At the Campaign to Protect Rural England (CPRE) HQ in London, my thanks are especially due to Oliver Hilliam, librarian and archivist. He spent a lot of his time pointing me in the right direction into the relevant CPRE archives, and also provided me with a desk – and decent coffee – during the time I spent in London. Thanks are due to staff at the Museum of English Rural Life, University of Reading (where the bulk of CPRE archives are kept).

At the Cumbria Record Office in Kendal (where the greater part of FLD archives are kept), Peter Eyre and his colleagues are to be thanked for their help, and especially for the suggestion that he would commission digital copies to be made of the unique set of over 100 original black and white photographs especially made for FLD in 1938, many of which appear in this publication. Also thanks to the Fell and Rock Climbing Club for granting me access to their archives – which are also lodged at Cumbria Record Office, Kendal.

At Lancaster University's Centre for North-West Regional Studies, I should particularly like to thank the following people: Firstly, Angus

Winchester and Alan Crosby for their positive advocacy for publication of the book, their willingness to read and make very helpful and constructive comments on the first draft manuscript, as well as for volunteering to write a Preface. Then Jean Turnbull for her professionalism and enthusiasm and her major role in overseeing the conversion of the draft manuscript into a publishable book with suitable illustrations; and lastly, but certainly not least, Christine Wilkinson, whose invidious task was to convert my initial draft manuscript into a professionally-turned out master document ready for the publishers.

    Finally, a very special thank you is due to Devoke Spence, one of Kenneth Spence's daughters. She kindly agreed for me to visit and talk with her on several occasions. I enjoyed her company and her hospitality during which time she willingly shared memories of her younger days and especially of her father. It is nice to know, and fitting, that she, and her sister Whillan, were two of the very first enrolled members of FLD.

Abbreviations

CPRE – Council for the Preservation of Rural England (now Campaign to Protect Rural England)

CTC – Cyclists' Touring Club

ELDA – English Lake District Association

FRCC – Fell and Rock Climbing Club

FLD – Friends of the Lake District

LDDS – Lake District Defence Society

LDFE – Lake District Farm Estates

LDNPA – Lake District National Park Authority

LDNRA – Lake District National Reserve Association

LDNRC – Lake District National Reserve Committee

LDSS – Lake District Safeguarding Society

NPC – National Parks Commission

SCAPA – Society Checking the Abuses of Public Advertising

SCNP – Standing Committee for National Parks

YHA – Youth Hostels Association

Foreword

The Lake District is one of the most exciting assets of England and Wales. The Friends of the Lake District strive to be its praetorian guard. Amidst the greed and materialism which sadly dominate our lives, bringing us all to the edge of self-destruction, it has become evident that we are part of a generation which knows the immediate price of everything but the value of all too little. No price can be put on the qualitative inheritance of the Lake District.

For two centuries it has been threatened by those with little vision who have endangered it with proposed developments which could have eroded and ultimately destroyed the very qualities that make it unique. Paradoxically, they could have irretrievably damaged the kernel of what provides the foundation for appropriately harmonised sustainable economic activity, not least the tourist trade.

Thank God that since the nineteenth century there have been heroes who, usually with few resources other than their own personal money, force of argument and tireless irrepressibility, have fought to make safe for us what today we are able to love and enjoy. These people were the pioneers of the Friends of the Lake District, the Campaign for National Parks, the Campaign to Protect Rural England, the Youth Hostels Association, the Ramblers' Association and the National Trust. We must never take their selfless dedication for granted. The imperative is to take that vision and commitment as the inspiration for our own relentless and effective determination in the same cause. The dangers will not go away.

Sinister materialist pressures, with their stressful consequences and the creeping suffocation of spiritual values by cultural and environmental homogeneity, make the Lake District more indispensably relevant than ever. The nation desperately needs the complete contrast, challenge, space for reflection and inspiration that it presents. Our eyes needs to be lifted, our lungs filled, our spirits renewed and our physiques tested.

What has been achieved since Victorian times, not least the establishment after the Second World War of the National Park, did not happen by accident. I am therefore delighted that in our 75th Anniversary year the Friends of the Lake District have published this fascinating and strikingly well researched account of the first years, written by John Cousins. The author deserves our warmest appreciation.

I am glad that the publication is dedicated to two outstanding zealots of the saga, Kenneth Spence and Henry (Hal) Symonds. Together with their collaborators they have helped to safeguard for all of us the healthy survival of this precious gem. We must never yield in our determination to keep safe what they achieved.

Lord Judd, February 2009

Preface

Alan G. Crosby and Angus J.L. Winchester

Writing in the early years of the eighteenth century, Daniel Defoe described the landscape of southern Cumbria in vivid terms: 'Here, among the mountains, our curiosity was frequently moved to enquire what high hill this was, or that. Indeed, they were, in my thoughts, monstrous high ... nor were these hills high and formidable only, for they had a kind of unhospitable terror in them ... Westmoreland [is] a country eminent only for the wildest, most barren and frightful of any that I have passed over in England'. Though his language was journalistically exaggerated, Defoe's sentiments echoed those of almost any sensitive soul from the south three centuries ago – the Lake District and its landscape were to be shunned and passed by as fast possible en route to the 'pleasant, rich, fruitful and ... populous' vale of Eden.[1]

Yet only half a century after Defoe's damning judgment was passed, Father Thomas West published the first tourist guide to the Lake Counties, and by the 1840s Wordsworth was denouncing the invasion of visitors and aspiring residents who, he considered, would destroy all that was precious in the landscape, culture and identity of his native soil. This dramatic reversal of earlier perceptions of mountain and wilderness was intimately associated with the new aesthetic constructs of the mid-eighteenth century, part of the same trend which saw more ambitious travellers seeking the awe-inspiring scenery in Switzerland and the Pyrenees as well as, or even instead of, the Classical vistas of Naples or the sophisticated salons of Paris or Florence. But, as was quickly apparent to Wordsworth and his circle, the popularity of the mountains and lakes, crags and torrents, was inexorably eroding the very identities which people sought. The commercialisation of lake shores, residential development on rocky slopes, or tripperish excursions to tourist attractions – all sullied the beauty of the scene.

Wordsworth and his fellows had good reason to fear the worst. In July 1831 the celebrated garden writer John Claudius Loudon visited Windermere and wrote in his magazine columns that

The lake district [*sic*] ... is, by its varied surface, rocks, and waters, admirably suited for the summer residences of persons engaged in business in towns; and as soon as railroads are completed between London and the larger manufacturing towns of the north, including Lancaster and Carlisle, an event which must inevitably take place before ten years have elapsed, we hope to see the hills thickly studded with villas and cottages from their bases to their summits. This seems to us the second step in the progress of the application of the lake scenery to the purposes of human use and enjoyment.[2]

The use of the area for agriculture and timber had been, in Loudon's view, the first step, while the third would be the harnessing of the superabundant water-power of the district for mills and industry. Loudon, a prolific and widely-read journalist, was prominent in the shaping and moulding of contemporary good taste. Given such sentiments from one so well-placed to promote his views, it is apparent that the potential for dramatic and threatening change was real and immediate.

The 1830s and 1840s may therefore be seen as a crucial to the emergence of a conservationist or preservationist agenda among those highly articulate and deeply committed devotees of the Lake District. Theirs was an increasingly vocal call to protect and guard the landscapes which the Loudons and their ilk saw as ripe for exploitation. After the mid-1840s, as the pressures upon the Lake District grew with the arrival of the railway at Windermere, it was impossible to ignore this numerically small but disproportionately influential group, whose conservationist message was proclaimed in newspapers and other media.

The Lake District was only one of many landscapes which were perceived as being under threat from intrusive development in the nineteenth century. In the early 1830s, for example, the philosopher and political economist John Stuart Mill, in alliance with a group of landowners, had vigorously opposed the planned route of the London to Brighton Railway through the Vale of Mickleham between Leatherhead and Dorking in Surrey. Mill argued that the landscape of Box Hill was 'unrivalled in the world for exquisiteness, combined with accessibility', and the plan was dropped. When a railway was eventually built through the Mole Gap, much of it was in tunnel and the rest carefully landscaped.[3] More famously, in the 1860s and 1870s John Ruskin had lambasted the railways, the quarrying industry and the filthy pollution of furnaces and limekilns which violated the beauty of the White Peak of Derbyshire. His outrage at the building of the Midland Railway through Monsal Dale in the mid-1860s epitomises a stark and bitter conflict between 'progress' and 'landscape'. Explaining how the landscape was of such beauty that 'you might have seen the Gods there morning and evening', he thundered that 'You [the Company] cared neither for Gods nor grass, but cash ... You Enterprised a Railroad through the valley –

you blasted its rocks away, heaped thousands of tons of shale into its lovely stream. The valley is gone and the Gods with it; and now, every fool in Buxton can be at Bakewell in half-an-hour, and every fool in Bakewell at Buxton'.[4]

But protesting and campaigning of this sort essentially tackled immediate and short-term causes. It did not address the more fundamental questions about the longer-term status of entire areas, or their ownership, administration and management. What could be done, in a society governed primarily by laissez-faire principles, to tackle the much wider issues of development control and land use planning which would be required? The evolving debate over conservation increasingly focused on the contrasts of public versus private ownership, voluntary action versus compulsion, and the freedom to roam and enjoy access versus the hitherto inalienable right for private owners to do what they wished with their estates. In the later nineteenth century were first articulated the ideas and arguments which led, 70 years later, to the designation of the first English and Welsh national parks

There were clear precedents elsewhere in the world, for in some countries governments had taken direct action towards landscape protection. As early as 1832 the federal government in the United States had set aside land around the scenic and natural wonders of Hot Springs, Arkansas, as a protected park, and in 1864, during the American Civil War, President Lincoln signed an Act of Congress which transferred the Yosemite Valley and the nearby giant sequoia groves to the ownership of the state of California on the condition that 'the premises shall be held for public use, resort, and recreation [and] shall be inalienable for all time'. In 1872 the Yellowstone National Park in Montana was created, arguably the first such formal designation in the world.[5] Other countries followed suit: Australia (1879), Canada (1885), New Zealand in 1887, Sweden (1909), and Switzerland (1914). Thus, the concept of the national park was crystallising across what might loosely be described as the Anglo-Saxon world in the 1860s and 1870s, and this unquestionably had a strong influence upon the conservationist lobby in the Lake District.

It has often been remarked, however, that national parks in this country (as they emerged in the 1950s) differ from those elsewhere in the world. Far from conforming to the conception of a national park as an untamed wilderness, those in Britain are settled and worked landscapes, in which most of the land is in private ownership and resident communities exploit the local resources to make a living. What sets them apart from other areas is their perceived cultural value to the nation, whether that value is aesthetic, recreational or conservational. National parks can thus be thought of as private land protected for the public good. They become, in Wordsworth's famous phrase about the Lake

District, 'a sort of national property, in which every man has a right and interest who has an eye to perceive and a heart to enjoy'.[6]

But that is only part of the story: upland areas like the Lake District and the Peak District have also been perceived as 'national property' in a utilitarian sense. High rainfall and deep, dammable valleys combine to make the uplands an obvious source of water supply for thirsty conurbations; poor marginal land can contribute more to the national economy if planted with conifers; today, windswept hills are ideal locations for wind farms generating clean energy. The very rocks themselves are a valuable resource – granite and slate in Cumbria, limestone and gritstone in Derbyshire and the Yorkshire Dales. What is more, as Wordsworth identified with clarity almost two centuries ago, the tourist potential of wild and beautiful landscapes itself contains the seeds of the destruction of what is perceived to be beautiful. The economic imperative to build roads, car parks, visitor attractions and hotels sits uneasily beside the desire to retain natural beauty. A tension between conflicting demands on the resources of an iconic landscape thus lies at the heart of the Lake District and other national parks and the organisation which is the subject of this book, the Friends of the Lake District, has never been far from the centre of the contest.

The conservation movement within which the Friends of the Lake District has been a major player has a number of different historical strands. As already noted, a long-term perspective shows that the conservation movement is a product of the sea-change in attitudes to the environment which took place in the mid-nineteenth century. If we examine that more closely, we see that the dominant paradigm from the sixteenth century to the mid-nineteenth had been 'improvement', the idea that the land was there to be tamed, reclaimed and made productive. In upland areas such as the Lake District that implied enclosure of fells and moors, to allow such land as was improvable to be reclaimed. When the process of enclosure was at its peak, in the early nineteenth century, the lower slopes of the fells were transformed as former common land was brought under cultivation. The plough, in the words of the agricultural pioneer, John Christian Curwen of Workington, writing in 1812, was carried 'much nearer heaven than what was ever dreamed of a few years ago'.[7]

But the taming of wild hillsides through enclosure coincided with a yearning for wild places, seen in the 'discovery' of the Lake District and the love affair with the fells which Wordsworth and the Romantics had already done so much to instil in the national consciousness. By the 1860s the practical consequences of the new mood were becoming visible. Thus, one response to urban growth and industrialisation was a desire to preserve access to remaining open spaces for amenity and recreation. The Commons, Open Spaces and Footpaths Preservation Society was founded in 1865 and a series of statutes, starting with the Metropolitan Commons Act of 1866, increasingly saw common land as public space to be preserved as the lungs of the nation, rather than as a utilitarian resource.

The first battles – laboratory experiments in applied conservation – were fought far from the Lake District. Public outcries against the possible enclosure of Wimbledon Common, Hampstead Heath and Putney Heath for sale as building land had prompted the formation of the Society and the passing of the 1866 Act. In a comparable development, the two Epping Forest Acts of 1878 placed 6,000 acres of ancient woodland in the ownership of the City of London, and guaranteed its management as public open space in perpetuity. The conflict of 'building plots versus recreational space' demonstrated the sharpness of the contrasts. In the terminology used by Christopher Smout when discussing changing perceptions of the environment, a concentration on the 'use' to which resources might be put yielded to a new paradigm, the 'delight' which could be obtained from experiencing the natural world.[8]

The drive towards public access and recreation started in the context of the metropolitan commons of south-east England but it had become a national movement, fusing with the Romantic love of the northern hills, by the early twentieth century. Rambling, a term which can be used as shorthand to encompass a wide range of outdoor pursuits, had become a powerful driving force by the 1920s, particularly in the towns of industrial northern England in whose backyard the Lake District, the Peak District and the Yorkshire Dales lay. A large and socially diverse population now felt that they had a claim on the open spaces of the uplands. In parallel with the rise of outdoor recreation there arose a separate but no less fundamental change in attitudes towards the environment.

A growing awareness of the fragility of ecosystems and a desire to protect wildlife formed a second strand in the shift from 'improvement' to conservation. In many of those northern industrial towns naturalists' clubs and societies were formed in the late Victorian period, where those who laboured and toiled in mills and foundries during the day sought escape, and intellectual satisfaction, in the study of the birds, plants, invertebrates and fungi which could be found on the moors and mountains of the rural hinterland. Nationally, the heightened awareness of the natural world which resulted from exploration across the globe was matched by the detailed investigation of Britain's own environments – the lonely slopes of Teesdale, the ancient woodlands of Dartmoor, the high fells of the Lake District, the fens and broads of East Anglia. Many of those landscapes were already threatened by agricultural change, industrial development and urban growth. In the years after 1880 these forces came together in the uplands, where aesthetic, ecological and recreational imperatives collided with commercial and utilitarian pressures promoting reservoir construction, road building, villa-type housing and afforestation.

The conservation movement is often thought of in terms of landscape aesthetics and ecology. Yet, since its discovery in the eighteenth century, the Lake District had also been seen as somewhere that was socially and culturally distinctive. Lake District rural communities were viewed as morally superior, preserving an older way of life that was free from the negative impact of the modern, industrialised age. Wordsworth's famous description of the heart of the Lake District as an 'almost visionary mountain republic ... a perfect Republic of Shepherds and Agriculturalists' was well-known and influential. Around 1903 Canon H. D. Rawnsley, vicar of Crosthwaite and one of the co-founders of the National Trust, erected a monument on Lonscale Fell, near Keswick, to two local shepherds. Writing of the memorial, Rawnsley hoped that it would teach those who passed it that 'our Cumberland mountains still as of old breed men of high purpose and noble endeavour; and that still, from following the sheep, God calls His chosen ones by lives of kindliness, simplicity and straightforward goodness, to guide their brothers in the path of duty, righteousness and truth'.[9] Rawnsley's hyperbole may have taken the idea of the 'moral purity' of mountain peoples to extremes but it encapsulated the notion that the Lake District's special qualities extended beyond landscape to the farming communities themselves.

Such ideas were powerful, particularly in the minds of the educated middle classes, by the early twentieth century. As economic pressures threatened the survival of hill farms, another strand in the conservation movement was the preservation of traditional farming – and farmers. The importance of hill farming in both creating the fabric of the Lakeland landscape and giving the region a distinctive rural culture was recognised and is reflected in the role of Friends of the Lake District, through its company Lake District Farm Estates, in buying up hill farms, not only to protect the environment from development but also in an attempt to preserve the traditional way of life. Like the National Trust, the Friends became closely involved in the practical management of landscape protection, moving from a campaigning and publicising role towards one which represented direct intervention in the land market and the use of ownership to control and influence development.

This welcome book charts the background and origins of the Friends of the Lake District, beginning with its immediate forerunners, the bodies which were created as part of attempts, from the 1870s onwards, to prevent unseemly and inappropriate developments in this lovely landscape. It also traces the growing campaign for the creation of national parks from the 1920s, when urban expansion, increasing concern for nature conservation and the outdoor movement combined to force a national debate on the future of the countryside, and culminates with the founding of the Lake District National Park in 1951, the goal for which so much ink had been expended, so many campaigns fought, and so many eloquent speeches made.

The book thus spans the history of the conservation movement itself, from individual protests, via group campaigns, to the emergence of institutional and state-sponsored strategies. As the last part of the book demonstrates, designation of a National Park was not in itself a solution: the debates, the controversies and the campaigns carried on, and flourish to this day. That is how it should be, for ideas are constantly evolving, public perceptions and expectations are fluid and sometimes fickle, commercial and social pressures do not diminish, and the philosophies of conservation and its political and economic context are continuously revisited and reappraised by observers and participants.

But the story of conservation in the Lake District lies at the heart of any analysis of the movement nationally. Nowhere has seen so many high profile battles, so many celebrity participants, and so much passion generated over so long a period. It is timely, therefore, to look at the history of one of the leading players on that dramatic stage, the Friends of the Lake District, and to consider the personalities and the principles which shaped its existence across the middle decades of the twentieth century.

Notes

[1]   Daniel Defoe, *A tour through the whole island of Great Britain* (first pub.1724–1726; this edn London: Penguin 1979), pp. 549, 550, 551.

[2]   John Claudius Loudon (ed. Priscilla Boniface), *In search of English gardens: the travels of John Claudius Loudon and his wife Jane* (London: Century/National Trust, 1988), pp. 75–76.

[3]   Peter Brandon, *The North Downs* (Chichester: Phillimore, 2005), p. 203.

[4]   Trevor Brighton, *The Discovery of the Peak District: from Hades to Elysium* (Chichester: Phillimore, 2004), pp. 190–191; it is often pointed out that the viaduct across Monsal Dale is now regarded as a magnificent *asset* to the landscape, and that conservationists were foremost in the unsuccessful fight against the closure of the railway in 1968.

[5]   For the context of the American experience see Wilbur Zelinsky, 'The imprint of central authority', ch.16 in Michael P. Conzen (ed.), *The Making of the American Landscape* (New York and London: Routledge, 1980).

[6]   William Wordsworth, *Guide to the Lakes*, ed. E. de Selincourt (London: Frances Lincoln, 2004), p. 93.

[7]   J. C. Curwen, 'President's Report', *Proceedings of Workington Agricultural Society 1812*, p.107. For this period see I. D. Whyte, *Transforming Fell and Valley: landscape and Parliamentary enclosure in north-west England* (Lancaster: CNWRS, 2003).

[8]   T. C. Smout, *Nature Contested: environmental history in Scotland and northern England since 1600* (Edinburgh: Edinburgh University Press, 2000), pp. 7–36.

[9]   H. D. Rawnsley, *Lake Country Sketches* (Glasgow: James MacLehose, 1903), p. 165.

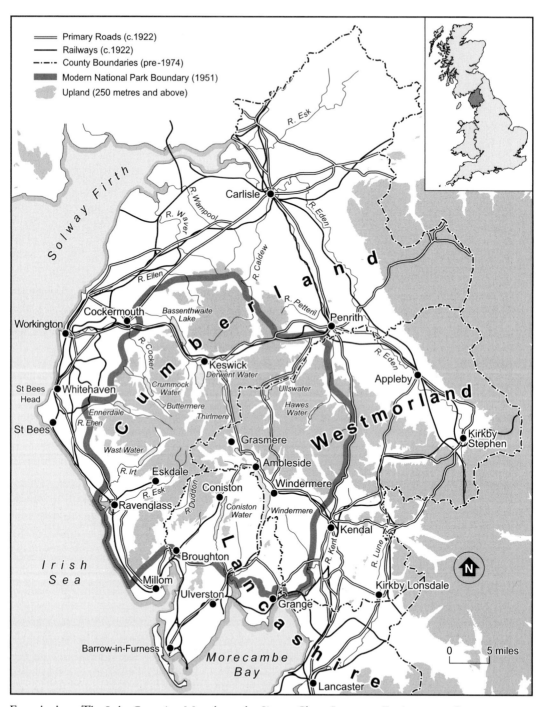

Frontispiece: The Lake Counties. Map drawn by Simon Chew, Lancaster Environment Centre.

Introduction

The case for the protection of the Lake District as a national park ... is an extraordinarily strong one ... But the only hope is in the driving force of a well informed and well organized public opinion. For though the problem is complex and difficult, and the general principles can only be applied by experts and through technical knowledge, yet the main thing which we all want is clear; hence the importance of some thoroughly national group of Friends of the Lake District, to supply the emotional impetus without which skill and knowledge win no victories.

Reverend H. H. Symonds, *Walking in the Lake District,* p.286.

The number of publications on the Lake District is huge and increasing in numbers every year. Many of them have become timeless classics: for example, Wordsworth's *Guide to the Lakes*; the Wainwright Fell Walking Guides; Norman Nicholson's many books – including his poetry; the two-volume histories of the National Trust in the Lake District; the illustrated books of W. Heaton Cooper; and H. H. Symonds' two books on walking and afforestation in the Lake District. Thus, this publication is hardly tackling a new subject.

So, why yet another book on the Lake District? What it seeks to do is to fill an important – and I think significant – gap in the history of those individuals and groups of people who joined together to organise concerted action to conserve and protect what they felt to be one of the best mountain landscapes in the British Isles, the English Lake District. This book is a history of the foundation and early years of one of the most important and influential of those groups. Friends of the Lake District (FLD) was formed in 1934. Many of the people who were responsible for its foundation and consolidation all those years ago were also very influential in helping to campaign for the creation of national parks during the 1930s and 1940s, at a time when the topic was very low on the political agenda. The establishment of national parks in England and Wales under legislation passed in 1949 is a measure of how successful they were. The story of the origins and the early years of FLD has not been recounted before in any detail. Now that we tend to take the conservation movement and national parks for granted, it is, perhaps, a good time to tell this story.

It should be stressed that this book is *a* history of the early years of FLD, not *the* history. The aim is simple. It is to produce a book that is of interest to all those, including the current 7,000 or so members of FLD, who are curious to learn about the origins and early years of the organisation, other landscape conservation and environmental groups and their members, and the academic community. It is designed to be accessible and of interest to those members of the general public who know and love the Lake District – both those who live there and those who visit: not an easy task. And I must declare my hand. First, I am a fully paid-up life member of FLD. I share their overall aims and objects, while not necessarily agreeing uncritically with all their campaigns or tactics adopted. Second, the sheer volume of available primary and secondary sources has made it necessary to be selective in what has been included – and, therefore, excluded. However, I have tried to interpret these sources as dispassionately as is possible. Inevitably, I have had to exercise personal judgements on what I have written about and how I have written it. Such is the nature of writing about the past. But I hope that the end result is judged objective, of some interest and worth the effort. I hope it may also stimulate both further studies of these early years (and the leading personalities introduced in this story, especially Spence and Symonds) as well as new studies of the later periods in the long history of FLD.

The Lake District and its special characteristics

The Lake District National Park was established in 1951. At 866 square miles, it is the largest National Park in England and Wales. Yet it only measures roughly 30 miles from north to south and the same from east to west. This represents less than a half-hour journey on a motorway: you could easily walk across it in two days. There are only three mountains over 3,000 feet. On a world scale it is tiny. Why then has it attracted so many 'friends' concerned with conserving what they felt, and still feel, to be its special features and qualities? And what are the special features and qualities that make it worth having the highest landscape conservation value? Many writers have tried to capture them in words. For example, in answer to the question 'Why … does the Lake District have a higher international profile than the Peak District, or the Wye Valley, or Snowdonia, or even Dartmoor?', it is argued that the difference lies in the Lake District's unique core area and more importantly how it has been perceived:

> Its landscape is its dominant attractive feature: but what matters is not so much the geology or vegetation in themselves, as the ways in which the results of these characteristics have been represented, verbally

(especially), and pictorially, in ways that communicate a sense of something especially alluring and enthralling, capable of conferring mental and spiritual as well as physical benefits upon the discerning visitor.[1]

The combining of a physical description of a mountain landscape with cultural landscape values, literary associations, and qualities such as access to solitude and spiritual uplift is a common theme of many who have written about the Lake District. All of these factors combine to provide a special tourist experience which it has been deemed important to conserve in the face of increasing accessibility and technological change during the last 200 years. Thus it is this iconic core of the Lake District – and how it is seen and experienced – which is still the key attraction for many tourists to the region today, as it has been since the Lakes were 'discovered' in the late eighteenth century.

Another – if more prosaic – way of looking at this connection between landscape description, interpretation and values, and landscape use, change and conservation is to consider the list of special qualities identified and described in the Lake District National Park Authority's (LDNPA) Management Plan 2004.[2] These are:

Complex Geology – This includes the distinctiveness and rarity of its geology and geomorphology giving us the deepest lakes and the highest and most rugged mountain peaks in England.

Diverse Landscape – Natural landforms are overlaid with thousands of years of human activity dictated by topography, especially mountains and farmed and settled dales.

Concentration of Common Land – The National Park has the largest concentration of common land in Britain (and possibly Western Europe) with a continuing tradition of collective management, especially agriculture.

Unique Mosaic of Tarns, Lakes, and Rivers – They give the Lake District a quality of scenery and recreational resource found nowhere else in England.

Wealth of Habitats and Wildlife – There are a wide range of habitats and species of national and international importance.

Extensive Semi-Natural Woodlands – They add texture colour and variety to the landscape as well as being of national importance.

History of Tourism and Outdoor Activities – It is the birthplace of mountaineering; has a tradition of open access to the fells for walkers; has been popular with tourists historically for its special features.

Opportunities for Quiet Enjoyment – The tranquillity of the fells, dales and lakes give a sense of space and freedom.

Open Nature of the Fells – The open character of the uplands and the lack of modern development are especially important; it gives a sense of remoteness.

Rich Archaeology – The landscape reflects a long history of settlement and land use, including prehistoric and medieval periods.

Distinctive Settlement Character – There is a strong tradition of vernacular architecture based on local materials, especially rocks and slates for buildings and dry stone field boundary walls.

Celebrated Social and Cultural Roots – Many personalities, lifestyles and traditions are particular to the Lake District. These include those working in agriculture and traditional industries, writers, painters, and environmentalists such as Wordsworth, Coleridge, Ruskin, Turner, Rawnsley, Heaton Cooper, Ransome, and the Arts and Crafts Movement. The National Trust and the movement for national parks in England and Wales have their roots here.

These special qualities inform very precisely what are deemed the defining characteristics of the Lake District landscape. Therefore, they also help shape and define policies and responses that should be considered to secure its conservation for now and for the future. Note that we are dealing with what is termed a cultural landscape: that is, one in which the past actions of humans help define its special qualities. Further, it is not about freezing a landscape in its original or existing state: this is neither possible nor desirable. Put succinctly, it is all about landscape values, use, change, and protection – issues which provoke strong emotions. Beauty, as they say, is in the eye of the beholder; value judgements must inevitably be made; opinions will differ. Therein lies the potential for conflict; and therein lies the story of FLD through from its gestation and birth in the 1920s and early 1930s to the present day. The founders of FLD might have expressed themselves in a different fashion but they would have recognised the qualities outlined above that make the Lake District special. Indeed, as we will see, it was because they regarded the Lake District as special that they fought so tenaciously (with others) to get the area recognised as a national park.

It could be said that the measure of success in the landscape conservation movement – including organisations like FLD – is in what you do not see as much as what you do. For example, the following proposals have been considered in the past, but did not happen: new reservoirs for Wastwater, Ennerdale, the Duddon Valley, Winster Valley, Swindale and Borrowdale (Westmorland); a major hydro-electricity power scheme for Upper Eskdale/Dunnerdale; large-scale coniferous afforestation in Eskdale and Dunnerdale; high tension and rural overhead electricity pylons/wires and telephone poles/wires through and within the Lake District; major road schemes for the A591 through the Lakes, including a dual carriageway from Kendal to Grasmere (with bypasses of Staveley and Ambleside); road widening and straightening in many dales and mountain pass 'improvements'; large-scale visitor developments, and timeshare accommodation; ribbon development, especially in Ambleside, Windermere, and Keswick; and extended and extensive military use of parts of the Lake District. A large number of these proposals first occurred during the period covered by this book and therefore at a time before the area was declared a national park. In many cases these schemes did not go ahead due to the concerted opposition mounted by FLD and others. However, various changes to the Lake District landscape through schemes that FLD opposed at the time have taken place. Thus, disputes over landscape use and change run like a thread through the history of the landscape conservation movement, and therefore the early history of FLD. Time and again we will see how FLD challenged what it thought of as inappropriate changes in land use detrimental to the special qualities of the area. FLD was prepared to lobby, whether the proposed changes were on the large scale, such as road schemes, afforestation, overground electricity and telephone proposals, quarries and water abstraction and ribbon development, or on the smaller scale, such as litter, visual clutter and signs, and building design.

The outline of this FLD story

This story, therefore, is about what has been termed the conflict between 'use and delight'.[3] The book seeks to chart the history of this conflict through the prism of events leading up to the formation of FLD in 1934 and thence through the key events of the early years until the Lake District National Park was created in 1951. It begins by outlining the Lake District landscape and its changes, including the impact of road improvements and the coming of railways, during the late eighteenth and nineteenth centuries; its 'discovery' by early travellers; and the subsequent development of tourism during the mid-to-late nineteenth and early twentieth centuries. The important amenity groups, and the campaigns they undertook in the nineteenth and early twentieth centuries, are then considered. A description of the main amenity groups formed in the 1920s, out of which FLD emerged, then follows. It includes information published for the first time on the backgound to, rationale for, and detailed events leading to, the formation of FLD.

For the story of these early years, the central role played by Reverend H. H. Symonds, Kenneth Spence, Norman Birkett, Patrick Abercrombie,

Theo Chorley and John Dower is considered. Amongst these it is Spence, early on, and then Symonds, who were the key figures. The afforestation 'quarrel' with the Forestry Commission, and FLD's significant – and possibly decisive – input to much of the meat of what was eventually included in the 1936 joint Forestry Commission/Council for the Preservation of Rural England (now Campaign to Protect Rural England) (CPRE) agreement on afforestation in the Lake District is described in some detail. Other major campaigning issues, such as the impacts of road 'improvements' and ribbon development, the introduction of telephones and electricity, water abstraction proposals, and the military use of land in the Lake District are also considered. Finally, FLD was in the vanguard, with CPRE, of the campaign for national parks, and FLD figures, wearing different 'hats', played pivotal roles on the CPRE Standing Committee on National Parks during the 1930s and 1940s. Therefore, some key events leading up to the 1949 National Parks Act, via the Dower (1945) and Hobhouse (1947) Reports, are outlined. Consequent FLD and CPRE disappointments with much of the legislation, especially the lack of a strong National Parks Commission with enough influence, as they saw it, to secure future landscape protection of the Lake District and other potential national parks, are explained. However, it is concluded that, in spite of reservations held at the time, FLD did succeed, with other amenity groups, in holding the ring for the national park concept during the 1930s and 1940s and, importantly, they did succeed in their key objective of seeing them created.

Notes

[1]   C. O'Neill & J. K. Walton, 'Tourism and the Lake District: Social and Cultural Histories' in D. W. G. Hind & J. P. Mitchell (eds.), *Sustainable Tourism in the English Lake District* (Sunderland: Business Education Publishers Ltd, 2004), pp. 19–20.

[2]   *Lake District National Park Management Plan* 2004.

[3]   T. C. Smout, *Nature Contested; Environmental History in Scotland and Northern England since 1600* (Edinburgh: University Press, 2004), Chapter One.

1 Scafell from Crinkle Crags – Easter 1937. From FLD archive, reproduced by kind permission of Friends of the Lake District.

Before the Friends: 1760–1914

It was here in the English Lake District that many principles of conservation were first voiced and developed: indeed the history of conservation in the Lake District is to a large extent the history of conservation in Britain. As a result of Lake District experience it became generally accepted that uncontrolled exploitation of the countryside for economic ends could not be tolerated.

G. Beard and G. Berry, *The Lake District: A Century of Conservation*, p. 53.

The formation of FLD in 1934 did not happen in a vacuum, nor did it happen by chance; indeed, it was not the first Lake District conservation group to be established, nor was it even the first with a national and international membership. To better understand why and how FLD was founded, it is necessary first to describe in outline the Lake District landscape as it was during the late eighteenth and nineteenth centuries, together with the forces and reasons for change. It is also helpful to outline the changes in access to, and within, the area, associated firstly with road improvements and then with the coming of railways, which contributed to the development of the Lake District as a popular tourist destination. And finally, some of the early campaigns undertaken and conservation groups established during these years, to resist what was seen as undesirable landscape change, are considered.

Introduction

In the late eighteenth and nineteenth centuries major technological change and population growth throughout Britain occurred, with industrialisation radically transforming society. This population increase was concentrated in ever-growing towns and cities: at the same time rural depopulation took place in many parts of Britain. The north west region of England was a focus of this 'industrial revolution'. Conurbations and industrial centres emerged in south-east Lancashire. Further north, around the western coastal fringes of the Lake District, Barrow, Whitehaven and Workington also grew to be significant urban and industrial centres. The Cumberland coastal hinterland was a major regional source of coal and other minerals and with the coming of the road improvements and railways they were fully exploited on a larger scale than before.

Landscape use and change

The location of the Lake District in this far north-west corner of England, combined with its unique mountain landscape, and its resulting poor internal communications, had long secured its relative isolation, not only from the rest of Britain, but also within the region. Throughout the period from 1760 until 1914 most parts of the area – from its mountain core to its lower fells and dales – remained, in relative terms, an agricultural and rural backwater. But it was not a wilderness waiting to be discovered. It was already a landscape heavily influenced by man's activities over many centuries, both for agriculture and for rural industries. The valley floors and lower fellside intakes were already farmed where possible, any formal or informal land enclosure and consolidation having mostly taking place by 1750. However, Parliamentary enclosures of land came relatively late to the Lake District. There were three main periods, those between 1810–1819, 1820–1829 and 1850–1859. It was during this third late surge that most of the enclosures of fell land in the central Lake District took place. For example, Watermillock, Ullswater, in 1835; Applethwaite, Hugill and Troutbeck in 1842; Sleddale Forest in 1849; Kentmere in 1850; Hartsop in 1865; Loweswater in 1865; Ennerdale in 1872; and Matterdale in 1882.[1] The main end product of these enclosures was the creation of large rectangular fields with distinctive drystone walls over many of the fells. However, the rugged nature of the terrain enclosed, together with their poor soils and high rainfall, meant that little land improvement could actually take place on an economic basis. Many of these newly enclosed allotments were subsequently converted to coniferous forest plantations. Their often rectangular straight walls provided a sharp discordant boundary outline on the fells for the new plantations. Indeed this new landscape use and design would contribute to serious disputes in the twentieth century between FLD and the Forestry Commission – as the new owners of many of these enclosed fells. Thus agricultural enclosures in the mid-nineteenth century led to new property ownership rights. However, very large areas of the Lake District fells remained as unenclosed common land.

By the late eighteenth century there were already well-established rural industries in the Lake District. Stone and slate were extracted from small local quarries for farm buildings, houses, walls, and bridges, especially from the mid-eighteenth century. Minerals extracted included copper, lead, graphite, and tungsten. Woodlands were also a resource exploited for rural industries. Coppice woodland was particularly important in the Lakes, and especially in the High Furness area for charcoal and the local iron smelting industry. However, quarrying and mineral extraction – whilst having an immediate visual impact on surrounding landscape, in the form of waste tips and possible water pollution of becks and lakes – was mostly highly localised and mainly small-scale: it was also heavily dependent on prevailing economic conditions. But from the mid-nineteenth century, with the advent of railways, it became possible to consider the 'exporting' of stones and minerals to the wider world. As a result, there was pressure to enlarge some existing working mines and quarries and to look for opportunities to open up new ones. Therefore, pressures grew during the nineteenth century for new railways to be constructed into the heart of the Lake District. The Ravenglass & Eskdale Light Railway was one proposal that went ahead, the line being opened in 1875 (these days 'Ratty' carries many happy visitors and locals each year up and down Eskdale, rather than stones and minerals). However, there was already opposition to quarrying and mining on a larger scale, and to the building of new railways to service them.

The 'discovery' of the Lake District

To talk of the 'discovery' of the Lake District is itself indicative of a history of its relative isolation in Britain. It had had a number of early travellers and tourists before the eighteenth century, who wrote about and/or mapped the region. In the sixteenth century these included John Leland (1540), Christopher Saxton (1577), William Harrison (1580), and William Camden (1586). In the seventeenth century, John Ogilby's *Britannia* (1675) included four detailed road maps in the Cumbrian region.[2] At the end of the century, Celia Fiennes was one of the first 'curious travellers' to visit and write about the region, when she travelled from Lancaster to Carlisle, via Kendal, Ambleside and Penrith. She confirmed that the roads at this time were only suitable for packhorses, not carriages.[3] During the eighteenth century the region was visited more frequently; and with the coming of turnpike trusts, many roads were improved. Daniel Defoe came to the region as a part of his tour of Britain in the 1720s, but he was not taken with what he saw. A major period of turnpike trust road construction took place between 1739 and 1767 in Cumbria. In particular, the 1762 turnpiking of the road from Kendal to Keswick marked the beginning of improved access to, and through, the central Lake District.[4] However, Arthur Young's description of road conditions in his *Six Months Tour Through the North of England* (1770) showed that some turnpike roads were still in poor condition (see Map 1).[5] It was from 1770 that the number of visitors really increased, even if they stayed for a limited time and visited a limited number of

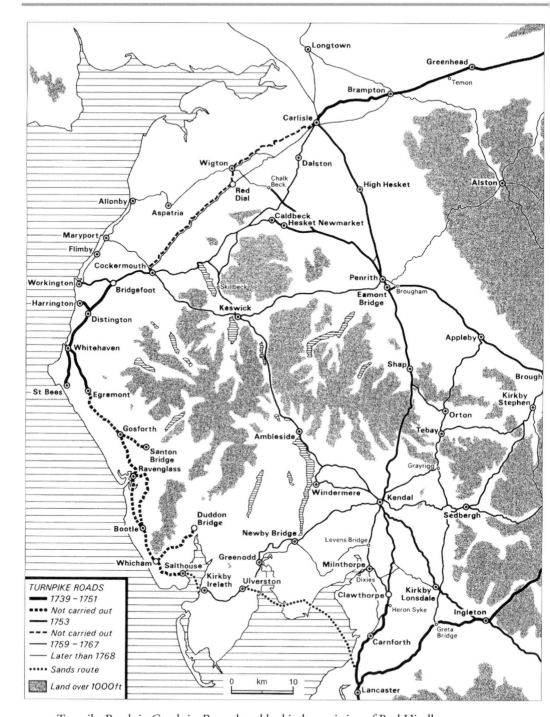

MAP 1 Turnpike Roads in Cumbria. Reproduced by kind permission of Paul Hindle.

places. Descriptions of Lake District scenery intended for general publication, and paintings inspired by it (for example, by William Gilpin), meant that the area became more known and celebrated for its intrinsic 'picturesque' beauty. Also, during the period of the Napoleonic wars, from the end of the century until the second decade of the nineteenth century, travelling by the largely few well-off people for the 'grand tour' on the continent became very difficult. The Lake District provided a good alternative. Arthur Young (1770) and William Hutchinson (1776) wrote about their journeys in the area, but it was Thomas West, in his *Guide to the Lakes* in 1778, who produced the most influential popular guide book that was specifically intended for visitors. In the second edition (1780), the poet Thomas Gray's description of his northern tour is included. The area was also popularised nationally through the influence of the 'Lake Poets', especially William Wordsworth, his sister Dorothy, and his associates Samuel Taylor Coleridge, Robert Southey and Thomas De Quincey. As well as his prolific output of poetry, Wordsworth also wrote a popular guidebook. His description of the Lake District landscape has not been bettered. He also first used the expression 'a national property' in relation to the area. This became the rallying cry for supporters of the national park movement in the early part of the twentieth century.[6]

The railway age and tourism

By the 1830s the tourist trade was well established in the three main urban areas of Keswick, Ambleside and Bowness-on-Windermere. In 1841 their populations were respectively 2,442, 1,281, and 1,479. Beyond that:

> the economic impact of tourism was, and long remained, negligible: an inn here, a carriage or boat there, a scattering of mountain guides. It took the arrival of the railways in the mid-nineteenth century to stimulate a level of economic activity that brought visitors in their thousands rather than their hundreds and really began to make a wider impact on the landscape.[7]

The opening of the Lancaster and Carlisle line in 1846 was pivotal to the changes that took place later in the century. It provided a direct west coast rail link between England and Scotland. The opening of the Kendal and Windermere line in 1847 linked the main line to a hamlet called Birthwaite on a hill above the lake. This inevitably led to pressures for new residential and commercial development around the new railhead. Birthwaite became Windermere. By 1861 Bowness and Windermere had overtaken Keswick in population, with about 2,987 as against 2,610. By the 1860s railway lines had surrounded the Lake District, and further branch lines into, and through, the Lakes were built: to Coniston (1859) and Newby Bridge (1869), as well as a line linking Penrith with

Workington, via Keswick and Cockermouth (1864). The railways had two main effects on the landscape. The direct visual impact depended on the exact routing through the countryside in terms of cuttings, bridges, embankments, and infrastructure, especially stations. The indirect secondary effect was on the surrounding countryside, especially the railheads and towns and villages within easy reach of the line. Wealthy people could consider buying land and having villas and large houses built either as primary or secondary residences near to the railway. Commuting from the Lake District to work elsewhere in the north west region became a possibility for a wealthy minority. Railways also encouraged people to move about more and further during their leisure. For the first time, it was possible to reach parts of the Lake District in less than a day from many parts of Britain.

Greater visitor numbers coming by train led to pressures for increased local accommodation and services. The potential for railways to carry goods and minerals as well as people was also part of their economic rationale – often the main part. Neither impact was universally appreciated. However, the summer season remained short – mostly July and August. By the late nineteenth century, growth in weekend excursion traffic had occurred, especially among the working classes of industrial Lancashire. However, the more lucrative tourists were still the middle and upper classes. They tended to have higher disposable income, and more leisure time. Some would stay for a few weeks. Many came from further afield in Britain. Furthermore, it has been estimated that 'as early as the mid-1870s up to one-eighth of Windermere's listed visitors came from overseas, especially the United States'.[8]

Many of these visitors, together with newer residents in their large houses and villas, formed the core supporters of the new hobby of yachting, especially on Windermere. Some were at the forefront as the founders of the new sport of rock climbing, especially in the more remote parts of the fells, in Wasdale, and Langdale. More hiking excursions – including ascents of the fells – were now described in popular guidebooks, such as Baddeley. Walking for pleasure became a major new leisure activity. By the early twentieth century the annual holiday for working people was well established. Working hours were also gradually reduced to allow for a 'free' weekend of leisure and many people enjoyed higher disposable incomes. Thus, from very early days, tourism in the Lake District depended on notions of solitude, tranquility and natural beauty, combined with respect for, and awe of, the natural scenery. Moreover, the 'visitor profile' mitigated against a demand for the kind of public entertainment facilities being provided at the burgeoning seaside resorts in the north west, such as Blackpool, Southport and Morecambe.

The first campaigns and conservation groups

The roots of the formation of FLD can be traced back to the last quarter of the nineteenth century. This was a time when influential figures such as Canon Hardwicke Rawnsley, John Ruskin and Robert Somervell began to challenge assumptions that all proposed landscape change meant progress. In particular, they identified the proposal put forward in 1876, to link Windermere to Keswick by rail, via Ambleside and Grasmere, as a particular threat. Robert Somervell, a Kendal manufacturer who lived in Windermere, led the campaign against the proposal. He issued a pamphlet, *A protest against the extension of railways in the Lake District.* John Ruskin wrote the preface. The campaign used moral and economic arguments, and involved national as well as local media. However, it was the economic arguments that won. Estimates of traffic were too low, and costs too high and for these reasons the scheme was not taken any further.

Also in 1876, the first Lake District group that could be called 'conservationist' was established. The brainchild of a group of Bowness and Windermere hoteliers, it was named the English Lake District Association (ELDA). Its objectives involved lobbying for the maintenance and improvement of roads and footpaths, and the provision of outdoor amenities without impairing the natural beauty of the area. Road maintenance was literally a 'hit and miss affair' as can be seen in the account of an American visitor to the Lakes who graphically recounted the poor condition of roads in 1855. He described a horrendous journey and finished 'I had rather travel from Maine to Georgia by rail, than from Grasmere to Windermere by stagecoach'.[9] ELDA supported the campaigns to prevent the extension of the railway beyond Windermere and to improve the increasingly insanitary state of Windermere, the result of increasing tourism.

Meanwhile, the huge increases in population in the north west during the nineteenth century led to increased demands for new and greater sources of fresh water supplies for the growing urban centres and their industries. The Lake District, with other locations, was viewed as a potential source of water for these cities and towns. In response to this need, Manchester Corporation undertook a search for possible sources in the Lake District. Ullswater was considered, but discounted, and Thirlmere emerged as the favoured option for a new water supply. By 1877 it was clear that Manchester Corporation would be seeking Parliamentary approval to construct a dam to increase the size of Thirlmere and to construct a supply pipeline to south-east Lancashire. Robert Somervell produced a pamphlet, *The Manchester and Thirlmere Scheme – An Appeal to the Public On The Facts of the Case.* As a result, the Thirlmere Defence Association (TDA) was formed, with Somervell as secretary. The

THIRLMERE PADLOCKED BY MANCHESTER
LOW TIDE.   AFFORESTATION

2 Thirlmere versus Ullswater 'access' issues. From FLD archive, reproduced by kind permission of Friends of the Lake District.

ULLSWATER. FREE ACCESS
NATURAL PEBBLY SHORE

committee included the Bishop of Carlisle, Ruskin, Carlyle, and Octavia Hill, as well as university academics and local landowners. Much of the national press, including *The Times,* gave the Association their support. However, although the campaign was able to delay the legislation, the scheme went ahead in 1879.

The Thirlmere defeat was a crucial moment in the history of the conservation movement in the Lake District. The campaign had been well supported and organised, but a change of approach was required. From these single-issue groups it was recognised that a more permanent organisation was required to campaign and lobby against future proposals for change deemed inappropriate. Thus it was that in the spring of 1883 the Lake District Defence Society was formed.

Canon Hardwicke Rawnsley is a seminal figure in the formation and management of the Lake District Defence Society (LDDS). Importantly, it was decided that LDDS should have a national membership, and this was achieved.[10] With this membership profile, LDDS was accused of being elitist, and its members mostly 'off-comers and outsiders'. However, the society made it clear that the Lake District was the 'property' of anyone regardless of his or her social background who cared about the preservation of its unique scenic beauty

By this time, popular guidebooks, such as Baddeley's, were emphasising – just as English Lake District Association (ELDA) had done – that this scenic beauty was the reason for its popularity as a tourist destination. That was reason in itself to resist any changes that caused potential harm to it. In fact between its formation in 1883 and 1914, LDDS did not suffer any major defeats. However, this may have been as much because many proposals for new quarries, mines, railways, roads and water abstraction were economically unrealistic, as because they were opposed by LDDS. Proposals – none of which went ahead – included water abstraction from the Duddon by Barrow's iron and steel works; a revised scheme for an extension of the Windermere branch line; the Buttermere & Braithwaite Railway; a mining railway in Ennerdale; and a new road over Sty Head Pass linking Keswick with Wasdale and the west coast. LDDS used its influence in two main ways: first, by launching public campaigns, including the use of petitions, letters, the press and periodicals; second, by using its network of contacts in local and central government, and the professions. Both these types of tactics would also be adopted by FLD after its formation.

LDDS also played a leading role in opposing the increasing number of rights of way closures. Many landowners, especially those with estates near to the larger towns of Windermere/Bowness, Ambleside and Keswick, objected to the use of these rights of way by the new visitors who enjoyed walking and hiking. LDDS worked with many of the locally-formed footpath societies to prevent closures. Rawnsley, wearing his many 'hats', is the key figure here. In 1885 he asked LDDS members to extend its objectives to support local commons and rights of way amenity groups (they had previously rejected this proposal). He also wanted LDDS to liaise with the Commons, and Open Spaces and Footpaths Society, which can claim to be Britain's oldest national amenity group, founded as it was in 1865. Its early members included John Stuart Mill, Sir Robert Hunter and Miss Olivia Hill. The latter two, along with Rawnsley, were the main founders of the National Trust in 1895 (see below). Although a national society, its early campaigns were almost entirely focused on securing public access to commons and open spaces in and around London.

This policy of extending its activities to include commons and rights of way issues was now adopted by LDDS. One Lake District footpath campaign, in particular, is worth outlining.[11] In 1883, Rawnsley was installed as Vicar of Crosthwaite, the parish church of Keswick. In 1885, two landowners closed important footpaths near to their properties in the Keswick area (in Fawe Park, in the north-west corner of Derwentwater, and Spooney Green to Latrigg, just north of Keswick). Rawnsley revived the Keswick Footpaths Association (formed in 1865) as the focal point of the campaign to get these footpaths reopened. The campaign received national coverage: protest meetings were held at local, regional and national levels. In 1887, a mass 'trespass', involving some 2,000 people took place on the disputed route from Keswick to Latrigg. Rawnsley did not go himself, preferring to keep in the background. The dispute came to court, at Carlisle Assizes, in July 1888. It was settled by mutual agreement, and public access to all the disputed rights of way was restored. By 1914 LDDS was largely defunct as a national organisation: but its leading members, including Rawnsley and Octavia Hill, still carried the flame locally on its behalf.

No survey of nineteenth century amenity groups would be complete without including the National Trust. Before the National Trust 'there was no national organisation which could realise the growing concern for the preservation of unspoilt privately-owned landscape and places of historical interest'.[12] Its origins lie in the commons, open spaces and rights of way movement, and support for the new amenity group came principally from Octavia Hill, Robert Hunter, and Hardwicke Rawnsley. They realised that one way in which future access to the countryside could be secured, other than by campaigning for it on a case-by-case basis, was to create an organisation that could fund the purchase, and receive bequests, of land and property to secure its long-term future on behalf of the public. Minds were focused in the Lake District when, in 1893, several sites came onto the market, including the island in Grasmere, and the Lodore Falls, in Borrowdale. Local authorities could not always be expected to buy such sites on behalf of the public. Furthermore, there was already concern about lack of public access to the eastern shore of Windermere, where many private villas with their estates had been developed, especially in the second half of the nineteenth century. In November 1893, Hunter, Hill and Rawnsley called a preliminary meeting to discuss the formation of a 'National Trust for Historic Sites and Natural Scenery'. After more preparatory work, the inaugual meeting of the new body was held in 1894. Olivia Hill moved the first, and historically important, constitutional resolution:

> It is desirable to provide means by which landowners and others may be enabled to dedicate to the nation places of historic interest or natural beauty, and that for this purpose it is expedient to form a corporate body, capable of holding land, and representative of national institutions and interests. [13]

3 The National Trust and Brandlehow opening ceremony, October 1902. Reproduced by permission of the National Trust.

The first National Trust Lake District public appeal occurred as a result of the death of John Ruskin in 1900. A memorial to him was erected on Friars Crag, Derwentwater (and after the death of Rawnsley, in 1920, the whole of Friars Crag plus Lords Island and part of Great Wood, Derwentwater were given to the National Trust after a public appeal).[14] The first, and successful, public appeal in the Lake District for land purchase occurred when the Brandlehow estate, on the western shore of

Derwentwater, was offered to the National Trust for £6,500. It was opened formally to the public in October 1902. Gowbarrow Park, Ullswater (750 acres) followed, and Gowbarrow Fell was opened to the public in August 1906. In 1908, another 100 acres nearly doubled the National Trust's Derwentwater holding; this was followed, in 1910, by Grange Fell, in Borrowdale (310 acres). By the outbreak of World War One, the following sites had been added to the National Trust's Lake District portfolio: Styhead Crag, Ullswater; Queen Adelaide's Hill, Windermere; the 'Borrans Field' Roman fort site, Ambleside; and the Castlerigg stone circle, east of Keswick. Finally, during World War One, successful public appeals were made for land to be dedicated to those who had died. In the Lake District, this included 1,000 acres of the Scafell area, including Scafell, Great End and Great Gable, a tribute to fallen members of the Fell and Rock Climbing Club. Rawnsley himself donated a viewpoint, 'Peace How', in memory of those from Keswick who had died.[15]

Thus by the First World War, the Lake District was recognised and established as a major tourist destination whose 'unique selling point' was its iconic mountain beauty. But this was now recognised as a fragile beauty. Increasing numbers of people felt that it needed protection. A necessary debate had been started about what should be protected, and why and how. This is, perhaps, the emerging nineteenth century conservation movement's major legacy, that the Lake District had now become 'a forcing-house for new ideas about the proper relationship between man, property, morality and the environment'.[16]

Notes

[1]   A. Winchester, 'The Farming Landscape' in W. Rollinson (ed.), *The Lake District Landscape Heritage* (Newton Abbott: David & Charles, 1989), p. 95.

[2]   See P. Hindle, *Roads and Tracks of the Lake District,* (Milnthorpe: Cicerone Press, 1998), pp. 66–71.

[3]   Hindle, pp. 73–74.

[4]   Hindle, Chapter 8.

[5]   Hindle, pp. 78–79.

[6]   W. Wordsworth (ed. de Selincourt), *Guide to the Lake,* (Oxford: Oxford University Press, 1977).

[7]   O'Neill and Walton, p. 28.

[8]   Ibid, p. 29.

[9]   Quoted in N. Nicholson (comp.), *The Lake District – An Anthology* (Harmondsworth: Penguin Books, 1978), p. 176.

[10] An analysis of nearly 600 members who signed up has been carried out. Fewer than 10% were based in Cumbria, more than 25% lived in London and the Home Counties; about 25% came from Lancashire, most from the Manchester area, and about 10% came from Yorkshire and the North East. Some 35 members were from

Oxford or Cambridge Universities; about 12 were Americans and there were 40 professors, 60 clergy and 34 masters from public schools, 18 of whom were at Charterhouse, but Eton, and Winchester were also represented. The headmasters of Uppingham and Rugby were members. The fields of literature and the arts were well represented, but so were Manchester merchants and Leeds industrialists. A formidable body of influence, expertise and capital was potentially available to the society. J. D. Marshall and J. K. Walton, *The Lake Counties from 1830 to the mid-twentieth century* (Manchester, Manchester University Press, 1981), p. 214.

[11] For a very full and detailed description and analysis of the Keswick footpaths dispute, see: D. R. Ellis, 'The Keswick Trespasses: working class protest or gentleman's agreement?', unpublished Diploma dissertation, Lancaster University, 2008.

[12] G. Murphy, *Founders of the National Trust* (London: Christopher Helm, 1987), p. 102.

[13] Murphy, p. 108,

[14] Murphy pp. 113 and 129.

[15] Murphy, p. 113.

[16] Marshall and Walton, p. 219.

4 Ennerdale from Green Gable. From FLD archive, reproduced by kind permission of Friends of the Lake District.

CHAPTER TWO

The genesis of the Friends: 1918–1934

We should embrace in our membership [of the Lake District Safeguarding Society] *those who do not purely come from the Lake District. We are too frightened of what the Keswick ratepayer thinks and forget that we have a national trust in our vigilance of this district.*

Kenneth Spence, Extract from a Letter to Mrs Rawnsley, 29 January 1929.[1]

The First World War was a watershed in more ways than one. If the nineteenth century could be summarised as the age of coal, steam and horsepower, then the early twentieth century saw the emergence of oil, electric power and the internal combustion engine as the main new forces for change. All of them had the potential for causing direct or indirect landscape change throughout Britain. The Lake District could not be isolated from the potential impact of these new technologies on its landscape, in particular the motor car and bus. Indeed Patrick Abercrombie – the main founder of the Council for the Preservation of Rural England – summed it up rather well, writing in 1926:

Improved means of communication are of course the chief engine by which urban decentralisation is brought about; indeed they are largely the cause of it: but they are also in themselves a cause of change in the countryside. It is only since the war that the normal method of approach to the country has been changed from the railway, by which it is accessible at fixed spots and at fixed times, to the motor car and bus, by which it is accessible by main, secondary, and local roads in all directions and almost continuously. The sudden outburst of the motor bus has caused a revolution in locomotion quite as remarkable as and indefinitely more swift than the railways. The immediate physical assault on the landscape by motoring can indeed in no wise be compared with the scars inflicted by the railways: but the complete permeation of the country is more thorough. There is no longer any real remoteness except in a few wild patches where there are no roads. [2]

Thus to the existing nineteenth-century threats to landscape character – such as major water abstraction schemes – there could now be added new twentieth-century ones; in particular, ribbon development and urban sprawl especially along existing and new roads in the absence of effective local planning controls, consequent pressures to improve and add to the road network itself, the growth of the national and local electricity grid and telephone network, and new large-scale state afforestation schemes. All of these new issues would be of central concern to existing and new amenity groups at local and national level.

As for tourism in the Lake District, it remained on a relatively small-scale with hotels and boarding houses in the existing towns of Windermere/Bowness, Ambleside and Keswick being favoured destinations. The growth of charabanc and coach travel led to more day trips and tours to and within the Lakes, but arguably the biggest change was in the growth of the middle- and working-class outdoor walking and camping movements exemplified by the newly emerging rambling groups (the Ramblers' Association was founded in 1934), and the establishment of associations of youth hostels (the Youth Hostels Association was founded in 1931).

Before the Friends of the Lake District – the major conservation groups

To better explain how FLD came to be formed in 1934, we can consider the various Lake District and national conservation groups which were already in existence or founded during the 1920s. Four bodies were instrumental in the debates which led to the founding of FLD: the English Lake District Association (ELDA); the Council For The Preservation Of Rural England (CPRE); the Lake District Safeguarding Society (LDSS); and the Lake District National Reserve Committee [later association] (LDNRC).

One of the most important key players in the conservation movement during the 1920s and 1930s was Kenneth Spence (1887–1944). Primary sources and records are clear and unequivocal about how pervasive and influential a figure he was.

Spence was born on 1 June 1887. He was a conscientious objector during the First World War. Crucially, he had his own private income from the family firm of Peter Spence Chemicals, near Chester. This meant that he could devote himself full-time to the various local and national outdoor and conservation groups of which he was a member. The family – his wife Gwendoline, and their two daughters Whillan and Devoke – moved to Sawrey House, Near Sawrey on 27 November 1925 (next door to Hill Top, the home of Mrs Heelis – better known as Beatrix

Potter).[3] As well as his close links with the various outdoor and conservation bodies, he was also well connected with the literary and musical worlds. Delius (the composer), Malcolm Muggeridge (journalist and author), and G. M. Trevelyan (historian) were among the names in the family visitor book, as were many others active in the pre-FLD period, people such as Patrick Abercrombie, Herbert Griffin, John Dower and James Cropper.

In the address given by John Dower at Kenneth Spence's funeral service at Manchester, on 16 February 1944, it was said that, amongst all the other organisations and movements he was involved with, 'for some ten years he was the core of the local and national effort for safeguarding the unique beauty of the Lake District, where he was first secretary and principal founder of the "Friends of the Lake District"'.[4] Moreover, in his outgoing FLD Presidential address at the 1969 AGM, Lord Chorley put the founding of FLD down to 'the enthusiasm and inventiveness of Kenneth Spence; he was the live wire at the beginning. I remember as though it was yesterday, going to his house to talk about it: he was an interesting man with an infectious enthusiasm.' He added 'it wasn't very long before the Reverend H. H. Symonds was roped in and that was possibly the most important thing that Kenneth Spence ever did.' [5]

Thus Kenneth Spence was already very active in a wide range of amenity groups regionally and nationally before 1934. He would now also be at the heart of the events leading up to the formation of FLD.

5 Kenneth Spence, 1934. From FLD archive, reproduced by kind permission of Friends of the Lake District.

1876 – English Lake District Association (ELDA)

As noted earlier, the ELDA was formed in 1876 with local hoteliers and local gentry as its core members. Its aims were to develop tourism and improve communications but at the same time to safeguard the scenery on which tourism depended. By 1922 its membership remained small – at 132 subscriptions. However, amongst these were James Cropper (owner of the major Burneside paper company, lord lieutenant of Westmorland, county councillor, and future chairman of the Lake District Safeguarding Society, the Lake District National Reserve Committee, and first chairman of FLD), Kenneth Spence, and Gordon Wordsworth (grandson of William).[6] The last formal meeting of ELDA was in 1938.[7]

1919 – The Lake District Safeguarding Society (LDSS) (also known as the Society for the Safeguarding of the Natural Beauty of the Lake District)

The LDSS, formed in 1919 by Canon H. D. Rawnsley, was the natural successor of the – by then defunct – LDDS, which was originally formed as a mass membership group in 1883. Crucially, it was now a purely local amenity group with membership by invitation only. It initially had 43 members, most of whom were local landowners. Its object was 'to endeavour by personal appeal, and by friendly means where possible, to safeguard the natural beauty of the Lake District', and it met once a year at most. Rawnsley died in 1920 and Mrs Rawnsley and Gordon Wordsworth became joint secretaries. The LDSS mounted a campaign in 1926 for a board of control over local development. By 1929 Kenneth Spence had become its secretary – with James Cropper as its chairman. Spence wanted a 'big tent' approach to be adopted by extending LDSS membership to the wider public on a national stage, but in this he did not succeed. However, this more radical approach became his rationale and blueprint for the kind of public landscape conservation group he wanted to see established, if not through an extended LDSS, then through an entirely new body. He assiduously lobbied and worked for this end – with any support he could muster from others – from 1929 onwards. His opportunity would come eventually come with the creation of the Lake District National Reserve Committee in 1929, out of which eventually emerged FLD in 1934.

1926 – The Council for the Preservation of Rural England (CPRE) (now Campaign to Protect Rural England)

The CPRE was founded in 1926 as a national amenity organisation that encouraged the establishment of active affiliated local branches. It was the brainchild of Patrick Abercrombie who became its first chairman after its formation.

Patrick Abercrombie (1879–1957) was born at Ashton-upon-Mersey and trained as an architect. In 1915 he was appointed as Professor of Civic Design at the Liverpool School of Architecture. He was a friend of Kenneth Spence, who himself was a CPRE founder member. His life-long interest in the Lake District was cemented when he acted as a joint consultant (with Sydney Kelly) for the *Cumbrian Regional Planning Scheme* of 1932[8] (Spence acted as secretary to the Cumbrian Regional Joint Advisory Committee which commissioned the report). Abercrombie was one of the main speakers at the rally held in Fitz Park, Keswick in mid-1934 that led directly to the formation of Friends of the Lake District. He was FLD's first technical advisor and planning

6 NPG x2401 Sir (Leslie) Patrick Abercrombie by Howard Coster. Half-plate negative 1944. Transferred from Central Office of Information, 1974 © National Portrait Gallery, London.

consultant from 1934 to 1938, and had become a vice-president of the newly-formed Youth Hostels Association in 1931. In 1935 he was appointed Professor of Town Planning at University College, London. During the Second World War he produced *The County of London Plan* (1943) and *The Greater London Regional Plan* (1944): collectively known as the *Abercrombie Plan*. Knighted in 1945, he was also involved in the post-war replanning of Edinburgh, Plymouth, the Clyde Region and Hull as well as being a leading light in the new town movement. He also had commissions overseas, including major plans for Hong Kong and Addis Ababa, Ethiopia. During all this period he kept close links with FLD.

CPRE's first full-time secretary was Herbert G. Griffin, who was also a friend of Kenneth Spence. Griffin owned property in Grasmere, although his full-time job as hon. secretary was based at CPRE Headquarters in London. Through the influence of Griffin as a key player during its early years in the 1920s and 1930s, CPRE came to see itself as a national organisation mediating behind the scenes between groups with conflicting interests. It preferred informal contact between itself and local and national policy makers to resolve issues rather than adopting an overt and public campaigning style. CPRE shared its vision of the future of the Lake District as a national park with FLD on its formation in 1934, but its wider brief and inclination to compromise would bring it into conflict with FLD from time to time.

In part these differences could be distilled and traced back to the very different personalities and philosophies of Kenneth Spence and Herbert Griffin. Spence regarded himself as a radical; Griffin saw himself as a conservative. Spence wanted a public national membership organisation to champion the Lake District cause, but Griffin preferred the more local and conservative methods as adopted by LDSS, working informally with local landowner interests behind the scenes to fight the Lake District cause. In the end Spence's radicalism and commitment to a more public campaigning organisation won the day. He was the driving force behind the launch of FLD and helped to establish it as the prime vehicle for the Lake District landscape conservation movement. However, it was Reverend H. H. Symonds who played an increasingly important role once FLD was established.

1929: The Lake District National Reserve Committee (LDNRC) – making the case for a National Park

Since its inception in 1926, CPRE had been lobbying central government to get it to consider the case for establishing national parks in England and Wales. The government responded in 1929 by agreeing to establish a select committee – chaired by the parliamentary secretary to the Ministry of Agriculture, Christopher Addison – to receive evidence from interested parties on national parks and make recommendations. As a result, CPRE convened a National Conference for the Preservation of the Countryside in Manchester on 9–11 October 1929.[9] It was also attended by other societies, including representatives of the National Trust, the Commons, Open Spaces and Footpaths Preservation Society, and local Ramblers' Associations. The following resolution was put and carried:

That the CPRE be entrusted on behalf of the interests there represented with the collection, preparation, sifting and collation of the best evidence in favour of a national park for presentation to the Select Committee.

Thus it was agreed to convene local 'national reserve committees' for those areas of the country likely to be candidates for national park status; these local committees would assemble the evidence for 'their patch'. This would then be collated by CPRE and form the core of its submission of evidence making the case for national parks to the Addison Committee.

That weekend a Lake District Session of the National Conference was held. It was arranged and convened by Kenneth Spence and a local committee at Ambleside. The case for the Lake District as a national park was put forward. A resolution was passed to establish a Lake District National Reserve Committee (LDNRC). It is worth quoting, since it set the agenda for the eventual establishment of FLD in 1934:

> That for the purpose of regional planning in the area, the authorities in the Lake District and the County Councils be recommended to establish executive joint town-planning committees; that the various societies interested in the preservation of the Lake District should be co-ordinated so as to concentrate effort and to avoid overlapping; that a small committee with power to co-opt be appointed from this conference to take the necessary steps to further these foregoing resolutions and to consider the question of the establishment of a preservation trust to secure the appropriate regional reservations and to prepare proposals to put before the Government Committee.

The convener, and secretary, of this newly formed LDNRC was Kenneth Spence – James Cropper became chairman. It included one representative each from a wide range of amenity and other organisations with a specific Lake District interest. They were the National Trust, the Society Checking the Abuses of Public Advertising (SCAPA), LDSS, ELDA, the Cumberland and Westmorland Antiquarian and Archaeological Society, CPRE, the Commons, Open Spaces and Footpaths Preservation Society, the Federation of Rambling Clubs, the Fell and Rock Climbing Club, and the two original North and South Lakeland Town Planning Committees. In spite of this broad coalition of interest groups, or perhaps one might say because of it, Kenneth Spence took the lead and was largely responsible for drafting and coordinating the evidence submitted by LDNRC, and thence by CPRE, to the Addison Select Committee making the case for a Lake District national park, with Patrick Abercrombie and John Dower providing a map of its potential area and boundaries.

The Addison Committee on National Parks reported in April 1931.[10] It recommended the setting up of National Parks Commissions for England and Wales with an annual budget of not less than £100,000 per annum for at least five years,[11] and the establishment of executive joint regional planning in the Lake District and some other potential national park areas. The Government chose not to act on the report due to the prevailing adverse economic circumstances. The country was suffering from a full-scale depression. Not until 1949 was a National Parks Act passed. However, Addison's recommendations formed the basis of the national parks movement during the 1930s and 1940s, in which FLD took a strong lead. Meanwhile, campaign tactics turned to attempts to get Addison's recommendation on executive joint planning committees established, especially in the Lake District.

1931–1934: the Lake District Three Counties Joint Planning Committee proposal; a failure to cooperate

Between May and December 1931 concerted action was taken by Spence, Griffin, and Abercrombie, on behalf of CPRE and LDNRC, to get Lancashire, Westmorland and Cumberland county councils to meet to consider forming a Lake District Joint Planning Committee as recommended by Addison. This was subsequently given legislative authority in the 1932 Town and Country Planning Act.[12] However, there were differences of view between Spence and Griffin about the tactics to be employed, including the need to have a meeting amongst key landowners in the Lake District, to get them on-side before suggesting a three counties preliminary meeting. This led to delays and by the time the county councils met in February 1932, Lancashire, especially, had become committed to its own plan. The proposals were rejected and when further initiatives were undertaken by LDNRC in February 1933 Lancashire did not even reply. CPRE tried again, but this time Cumberland County Council was lukewarm to the joint planning idea. Spence was now convinced that the only way forward was to extend membership of the LDNRC to the wider public both locally and nationally. He felt this would give greater weight to the campaign and lobbying for the full implementation of the recommendations of the Addison Committee. Thus the emphasis would soon change from seeking to get local joint regional planning to enforcing regional planning via a new, strong, centralised national park authority with powers to oblige local authorities to implement their new powers in the 1932 Town and Country Planning Act. Hence the proposal favoured and led by Spence – with the support of other key figures such as Patrick Abercrombie, John Dower, Norman Birkett, Theo Chorley and Henry Symonds – was to convert the LDNR *Committee* into a local and national public membership *Association.*

Spence articulated the reasons why this new amenity group was needed, and what its purposes were, in a talk given to BBC North Region on 17 August 1934, and summarised in an accompanying magazine article.[13] He said FLD had recently been formed, making it clear that 'it will perform work beyond the ordinary scope of a protection society, and outside the work of the Council for the Protection of Rural England and the National Trust have aimed at doing'. In the short term it would seek to create a compensation fund to help landowners and local authorities preserve 'those open spaces that make Lakeland what it is', and also support fellow organisations, especially the National Trust, in its *ad hoc* fund raising activities.[14] But its prime purpose was to lobby for 'the Government to put into practice the recommendations of the National Park Committee [in its Addison Report of 1929]' so that 'Lakeland will finally have one really local and at the same time national controlling body to care for it and protect it, and thus make it truly the first National Park in Great Britain'.

1934: the Lake District National Reserve Association (LDNRA) – Friends of the Lake District (FLD)[15]

Since their inception in 1931 it had become the custom for the Ramblers' Federation to have an annual public rally on the third Sunday in June. In 1934 this was organised for Sunday 17 June at 3.15 p.m. in Fitz Park, Keswick (see Figure 7). However, on this occasion, instead of confining the rally to ramblers, it was announced that Youth Hostels Association members and representatives of the Lake District National Reserve Committee would be joining the event. The declared object was 'to bring forward a proposal to form an Association to be known as "Friends of the Lake District"' (or 'Lake District National Reserve Association'). One of the leaflets produced to publicise the rally states in very small print that further particulars could be obtained from Mr Kenneth Spence, Sawrey House, Far Ambleside. On 14 June 1934, three days before the meeting, a substantial leaflet was published, explaining in detail why the new Association was necessary, and inviting the public to subscribe. It also included a reprint of an Appeal letter announcing the proposed launch of what was described as the Lake District National Reserve Association 'Friends of the Lake District'.

However, this leaflet and details of the rally do not reveal the degree to which Kenneth Spence drove the agenda behind the scenes to get all member organisations of the LDNRC on board. It was vital that all these various disparate groups and organisations – including the three county councils – should sign up to the leaflet's contents and the appeal letter to the press before the open-air rally in Keswick. Spence had at least the tacit, if not active, support of his LDNRC chairman, James Cropper, and there is crucial documentary evidence that he also had the key support of Patrick Abercrombie (as hon. secretary of CPRE). Spence worked against extremely tight deadlines. At the same time he had to deal with the real concerns expressed by Herbert Griffin (full-time general secretary of CPRE) about the rationale and need for this new group. The key events all took place during a very short period at the end of May and beginning of June 1934, and thus in somewhat of a hurry.[16]

Only on 25 May 1934 – some three weeks before the open-air rally was to be held – did Spence send out a letter on behalf of LDNRC to all committee representative bodies, enclosing what he called the final draft of the appeal pamphlet proposing to convert the committee to a wider public association to be known as Friends of the Lake District. He had largely drafted the leaflet himself, clearing it with Patrick Abercrombie beforehand, and also with John Dower, who provided the sketch map of the proposed national park area to form part of the leaflet. Two things shocked Griffin at CPRE. First, the original 'Spence' draft claimed that a three counties joint planning committee had already been set up. Second, and more importantly, he was

7 Poster advertising the public rally to launch Friends of the Lake District, 17 June 1934. From FLD archive, reproduced by kind permission of Friends of the Lake District.

very lukewarm about the whole idea of a new campaigning organisation, especially since a new Lancashire branch of CPRE had only recently been established, with Griffin, Abercrombie, Spence, and Symonds having had a major influence in getting it off the ground. At the very least Griffin thought there was room for confusion as to its relationship with the proposed new FLD.[17]

Griffin wrote to Spence and told him of his concerns. Spence then sent Griffin a letter dated 28 May in which he amended the draft, and indicated that Abercrombie (on behalf of CPRE) had already seen and approved it. He then asked if Griffin would arrange for the leaflet to be produced by CPRE printers. Griffin obtained written confirmation from Abercrombie that he had indeed approved the idea of forming the FLD, and also the contents of the leaflet. Spence – as secretary of LDNRC – convened a special meeting of LDNRC for Monday 4 June to agree the final text and the final arrangements for the 17 June open-air meeting in Keswick.

There followed a frantic exchange of correspondence, including telegraphs, between Spence and Griffin, in which they sought each other's help in getting the key organisations and individuals to sign the appeal leaflet before its planned publication date of 14 June and the announcement to the press. Typical of these exchanges is a letter from the

Membership is open to all individuals subscribing 2/6, and to societies paying an affiliation fee of a guinea, but it is hoped that Friends of the Lake District will send additional contributions to augment the fund.

A meeting of those who subscribe will be summoned in the near future at a suitable time and place.

Yours etc.,

(Signed)

DERBY, Lord Lieutenant of Lancashire
S. H. le FLEMING, Lord Lieutenant of Westmorland
WILLIAM EBOR
HERBERT CARLIOL
F. S. CHANCE, High Sheriff of Cumberland
F. C. SCOTT, High Sheriff of Westmorland
BALNIEL, M.P. for North Lonsdale
W. NUNN, M.P. for Whitehaven Division of Cumberland
OLIVER STANLEY, M.P. for Westmorland
GEO. H. PATTINSON, Chairman Westmorland County Council
ALFRED SUTTON, Chairman Cumberland County Council
JAMES TRAVIS-CLEGG, Chairman Lancashire County Council
CRAWFORD & BALCARRES, President Council for the Preservation of Rural England

ROCHDALE	T. A. LEONARD
MABEL HOWARD	GEOFFREY Le M. MANDER
S. H. SCOTT	HENRY W. NEVINSON
CHARLES TREVELYAN	EVELYN SHARP
G. M. TREVELYAN	ELEANOR F. RAWNSLEY
JOHN ASPELL	CHARLES ROBERTS
PATRICK ABERCROMBIE	ARNOLD S. ROWNTREE
W. F. ASCROFT	H. H. SYMONDS
R. NOTON BARCLAY	A. W. WAKEFIELD
NORMAN BIRKETT	GORDON G.
R. S. T. CHORLEY	WORDSWORTH
LAWRENCE CHUBB	GEOFFREY WINTHROP YOUNG

J. W. CROPPER, Chairman Lake District National Reserve Committee
KENNETH SPENCE, Hon. Sec. ,,   ,,   ,,   ,,   ,,
(Sawrey House, *via* Ambleside) to whom subscriptions should be sent.

CPRE President, Lord Crawford and Balcarres, to Griffin, dated 12 June 1934, a mere five days before the Keswick meet, which included the following: 'I have had a terrific long letter from Kenneth Spence, asking me to sign a document about the Friends of the Lake District. Is there any objection to my doing so?' On 11 June Griffin received the proofs of the launch leaflet from the Garden City Press, on 14 June Lawrence Chubb signed up on behalf of the Commons, Open Spaces and Footpaths Preservation Society, and finally, on 15 June Dower wrote to Griffin to inform him that he had received 2,000 copies of the LDNRA Appeal leaflet and intended taking 1,500 copies to the Lake District for the 17 June launch in Keswick. [18]

8 Signatories of members of the Lake District National Reserve Committee from the LDNRA/FLD launch leaflet. From FLD archive, reproduced by kind permission of Friends of the Lake District.

The public rally – Fitz Park, Keswick 17 June 1934

The rally was held, preceded by a short service held at 2.30 p.m. conducted by the Reverends C. H. Lewin and D. Garnett of Keswick and with a public address by the Reverend Philip Ashton of Carlisle. Addresses were given by T. A. Leonard (Chairman, National Council Ramblers Federations), Sir Charles Trevelyan, Prof. P. Abercrombie, Rev. H. H. Symonds (chairman, Merseyside YHA), Mrs. A. W. Wakefield (Lakeland YHA), and Mr W. S. Newell (Lakeland Holiday Federation).

The event was regarded as a success, and was widely reported in the local and national press. For example, the *Westmorland Gazette* of 23 June 1934 ran a very full article on the Rally, reporting that the resolution 'That this gathering of ramblers and lovers of the Lake District welcomes the formation of the Lake District National Reserve Association' was carried unanimously, and that:

A message was read out from the Prime Minister – Ramsay MacDonald – in which he said that such gatherings were greatly to be commended as they encouraged people to seek out the loveliness of the unspoiled country, and also helped to teach the sometimes

thoughtless townsman that it was his duty to leave its loveliness unspoiled in order that those who followed in his tracks might enjoy it also.

June-October 1934: the Friends of the Lake District is officially launched

Between June and October 1934, the groundwork for the formal establishment of FLD proceeded. A first LDNRA management committee was held in Windermere on 22 September. Kenneth Spence – now 'provisional Hon. Secretary' of the Association – reported that 530 individual members had joined, together with eight affiliated bodies. A draft constitution was prepared by Symonds, Spence and W. S. Ashcroft. The first meeting of the newly appointed and formed executive committee took place at the Council Chamber, Windermere on 19 October 1934. Two key extracts from the minutes are included below:

> Item 2. <u>Minutes of the Lake District National Reserve Committee</u>. It was decided that the Chairman read and sign the minutes of the LDNR Committee, which Committee is now incorporated in the Friends of the Lake District …

9 Founders at the public rally to launch Friends of the Lake District, Fitz park, Keswick, 17 June 1934. Front, left to right: H. H. Symonds, T. A. Leonard, Sir Charles Trevelyan, Mrs A. W. Wakefield, K. G. Spence, R. Taylor. Behind: Professor Abercrombie, Rev. Charles Lewin, W. S. Newall, J. W. Cropper. From FLD archive, reproduced by kind permission of Friends of the Lake District.

Item 6. <u>Title of Society</u>. It was decided by eight votes to two that the word 'association' be dropped and the new body [be] known as 'Friends of the Lake District'.

Where did the name 'Friends of the Lake District' come from?

10 FLD recruitment flier showing map of boundaries of proposed Lake District National Park. From FLD archive, reproduced by kind permission of Friends of the Lake District.

It is generally agreed that credit for the origin of the name 'Friends of the Lake District' is due to the Reverend H. H. Symonds. In his classic book *Walking in the Lake District*, Symonds said 'hence the importance of some thoroughly national group of Friends of the Lake District, to supply the emotional impetus without which skills and knowledge win no victories'. Whether he was the first to coin such a phrase is irrelevant; he was certainly involved in the gestation and formation of FLD, though it was not until the late 1930s that he moved centre stage, once Spence had resigned and left the District. In any case, no one could disagree that it was a far better name for a new campaigning group than the more cumbersome and anodyne Lake District National Reserve Association.

IF YOU WALK CLIMB OR CYCLE IN THE ENGLISH LAKE DISTRICT—

IF you would see its beauty preserved unspoiled—

IF you would safeguard its footpaths and public access—

IF you would prevent the construction of main roads over its mountain passes—

IF you would control all quarrying, mining and industrial activities in its area—

IF you would banish from it all litter, advertisement hoardings and unsightly petrol-pumps—

IF you would like any new buildings in its area to conform to local architectural traditions—

IF you would have the Lake District reserved as a National Park— JOIN "FRIENDS OF THE LAKE DISTRICT"

SEND YOUR SUBSCRIPTION (2/6 minimum) to the Hon. Treasurer, Sawrey House, via Ambleside.

"FRIENDS OF THE LAKE DISTRICT"

Minimum subscription (individual members): 2/6 per annum.

To the Hon. Treasurer, Sawrey House, via Ambleside.

I wish to become a Friend of the Lake District and enclose
£   :   :   , as my subscription for the current year.
£   :   :   , as a donation.   Date

Cheques and Postal Orders should be made payable to "Friends of the Lake District."

Name
Address

Members can obtain on application small enamel badge showing map: price 1/-.

Looking back at the early years of FLD, what stands out most today is how quickly this new amenity group made its own distinctive – if sometimes controversial – mark at both local and national level. From the start it began to set the agenda, by articulating and describing the kind of Lake District landscape that should be conserved and, as importantly, why. The FLD and key FLD players (sometimes wearing other 'hats'), took a leading role in a sustained push for national parks in general and the Lake District in particular during the 1930s and 1940s. After all, this was the main reason for its establishment. Founder FLD members such as James Cropper, Kenneth Spence, Henry (Hal) Symonds, Norman Birkett, Theo Chorley, Patrick Abercrombie, and John Dower were already well connected personally and professionally and had influence in many parts of the

11 James Cropper, first Chairman of FLD. Private Collection.

establishment. Further, there were existing strong personal links between key FLD players and national bodies such as the CPRE, the National Trust, the Commons, Open Spaces and Footpaths Preservation Society, the Ramblers' Association (formed in 1934 out of the National Council of Ramblers' Federations, itself founded in 1931) and the emerging national Youth Hostels Association (formed in 1931), as well as more local bodies such as the Fell and Rock Climbing Club (FRCC) and the Lake District Safeguarding Society (LDSS).

However, during those early years there were disagreements between FLD and other amenity groups, both locally and nationally, about the

2 A 'clutter-free' dale, Mickleden, Great Langdale. From FLD archive, reproduced by kind permission of Friends of the Lake District.

tactics to be employed to achieve their common aims. FLD set out to recruit any members of the public who shared the aims of the new society. From the start it explicitly included in its tactical armoury the potential use of high profile public campaigning and lobbying by its members and the wider public to achieve its goals. This was in addition to the more traditional, formal, low profile approach of *ad hoc* alliances with other amenity groups, meeting with and lobbying public and private sector organisations, and use of the media. Some thought this type of campaigning was not only too radical but was also counter-productive. Indeed, FLD was often pictured as a left-leaning, radical group of mostly 'off-comers' and outsiders. But the truth is that the key FLD players were well-educated middle and upper-class members of the English establishment.[19] And in many cases they were also landowners in the Lake District. They were, however, not afraid of employing a public campaigning approach as well as their networking abilities even at the expense of short-term popularity.

It was up to this new amenity group to deliver on its objects, including that of 'organising concerted action for protecting the landscape and natural beauty of the Lake District' and cooperating with 'any other body having interests or objects similar to the Objects of the Association'. As already noted, landscape changes resulting from the advent of the internal combustion engine, with the resulting dangers of unplanned urban and rural development (including calls for new and 'improved' urban and rural roads), plans for new modes of electricity generation and transmission, new large-scale state afforestation, and the continuing need for water abstraction and transmission for the cities and towns of the north west, had been under way well before October 1934. These, and other, issues already informed the existing Lake District conservation movement agenda. From now on they would inform the FLD agenda as well. The in-tray was full from the outset.

Notes

1   CRO (Kendal) WDX/422/2/8, Rawnsley Papers.

2   Patrick Abercrombie, *The Preservation of Rural England – The Control of development by means of Rural Planning* (London: Hodder and Stoughton, 1926), p. 11.

3   Sawrey House is now the Sawrey House Country Hotel and Restaurant.

4   *Kenneth Spence – an address given at his funeral service at Manchester, 16th February 1944, by John Dower, and printed for circulation to his friends.* Copy provided to the author by his daughter Devoke Spence.

5   See FLD *Report and Newsletter* 1969. Spence was actively involved with the following organisations:
     Fell and Rock Climbing Club – member from 1923, and their representative at CPRE Annual Conferences after its formation in 1926.
     Council for the Preservation of Rural England (CPRE) – a founder member (1926) and Cyclists Touring Club representative on CPRE National Executive Committee.
     Member of *English Lake District Association.*
     Member and then secretary of the *Lake District Safeguarding Society.*
     Co-founder and then secretary of the *Lake District Reserve Committee (LDNRC)* which thence became *Association* and *Friends of the Lake District* in 1934.
     Chairman of *Youth Hostels Association – Lake District Branch.*

6   CRO (Kendal) WDX 422/2/7 1922 ELDA *Report and Accounts.*

7   Assets included War Stock, and a parcel of land and access to Skelwith Force waterfall by Halfway House, Skelwith Bridge.

8   P. Abercrombie and S. A. Kelly, *Cumbrian Regional Planning Scheme* (London: Hodder and Stoughton, 1932).

9   See CPRE *Annual Report* 1929, pp. 72–73.

10   C. Addison *Report of the National Park Committee*, Cmnd 3851, HMSO, 1931

11   With the option – because of the current economic circumstances – of at least £10,000 per annum over five years provided and administered by Government Departments and a new National Advisory Committee.

12   CPRE File 232/2 now C/1/102/16.

13 ' The Future of the Lake District', *The Listener*, August 1934.

14   During 1934 the National Trust had launched its Buttermere appeal.

15   CPRE File 232/6 now C/1/102/20.

16   Ibid.

17   It is interesting to speculate what might have been the future for a new amenity group focused solely on the proposed Lake District national park area had CPRE branches also already been established in Cumberland and Westmorland as well as Lancashire. Today FLD is CPRE's representative for Cumbria.

18   Spence also won over a sometimes sceptical minority of FRCC committee members and eventually gained a clear mandate from FRCC to support FLD formation, and thence for FRCC to become a founding subscribing FLD affiliate. See FRCC committee minutes, 19 May, 14 July and 6 October 1934. CRO WDSO 163/Record Box Number Two' Minutes 1907–1947.

19   In early 1935, James Cropper (FLD Chairman) was owner of a major paper manufacturing company, in Burneside, near Kendal, and was also high sheriff of Westmorland and a member of Westmorland CC: Kenneth Spence had his own private income and was a company director; Patrick Abercrombie was a founder of CPRE and Professor of Civic Design at Liverpool University; Reverend Symonds was headteacher at the Liverpool Institute; Theo Chorley was Professor of Law at University of London and President of FRCC; John Dower had his own architectural and town planning practice; Norman Birkett was a KC; FLD president Lord Howard of Penrith was a landowner and member of the House of Lords, and at least two of them, Chorley (Kendal) and Birkett (Ulverston) were born in the area.

PILLAR FELL
BEFORE AFFORESTATION

13 Pillar, Ennerdale, before afforestation. From FLD archive, reproduced by kind permission of Friends of the Lake District.

CHAPTER THREE

The first major campaign – the afforestation quarrel: 1934–1936

The complex beauty of the Lake District is easily wounded, and it can suffer no greater wound than by this invasive, all-flattening steam-roller of afforestation for commerce. Public access is one thing; public access at the price of afforestation is another. To ask, as many do ask, for a national park, and then to be offered in the Lake District a 'national forest park', is to be offered a mess of pottage for a national birthright.

H. H. Symonds, *Afforestation in the Lake District,* page 69.

In this chapter, the course and outcome of the debate which raged between 1934 and 1936 over the Forestry Commission's plans for further afforestation in the central Lake District will be considered. This debate is particularly important because, first, it was one of the major items on FLD's agenda as a new independent organisation. It was therefore a major test of its mettle and lobbying methods in resisting what it saw as threatening, significant and undesirable landscape change.

Second, the nature, location and scale of these particular Forestry Commission afforestation proposals involved the continuation of arguably the single largest category of landscape change the Lake District faced in the twentieth century to date, notwithstanding the Thirlmere and Haweswater water abstraction schemes. The need, as the Forestry Commission saw it, for large-scale land acquisitions on economic grounds for timber production as a national strategic reserve implied wholesale landscape change in many parts of the area. Therefore, the issue of the proposed Hardknott Forest Park (following the earlier purchases of land in Ennerdale and Whinlatter for large-scale afforestation) would continue to set a precedent for future afforestation proposals elsewhere in the Lakes. This was perceived by FLD from the start as a huge potential threat, not only to the special mountain and fell landscape character and appearance – with questions of loss of public access to hitherto open dales and fells also to the fore – but also to traditional Lakeland sheep farming and the way of life with which it was inextricably associated.

FOR THE ATTENTION OF
THE FORESTRY COMMISSION

14 'For the attention of the Forestry Commission'. From FLD archive, reproduced by kind permission of Friends of the Lake District.

BLANKET OF COMMERCIAL SPRUCE
BY FORESTRY COMMISSION.   BASSENTHWAITE

Third, the issue opened up a major debate about the role of the state and its agencies in pursuing goals which were incompatible with the landscape protection of an area that had already been identified by the Addison Committee as a potential future national park. It was one thing to challenge the interests of local landowners and local authorities. It was quite another to respond to a major government agency, the Forestry Commission.

Fourth, it can be deduced from the documentary records that FLD, in spite of its disagreements over tactics and ends with CPRE, gave CPRE much of the detailed analysis and facts which the latter used in its meetings with the Forestry Commission, and which were instrumental in shaping many of the proposals which the Forestry Commission and CPRE agreed in their joint report in July 1936. Credit for this detailed analysis should be given to Symonds. He had a good knowledge of the terrain in question, as his seminal books *Walking in the Lake District* and *Afforestation in the Lake District* made clear, and an ability to marshal facts and arguments based on a passionate belief in the veracity of the case against the Forestry Commission because of the damaging landscape effects of unsympathetic coniferous afforestation. It can also be argued that without FLD's public campaign the outcome might have been further tipped towards the Forestry Commission's position.

And lastly, the so called 'red-line' maps drafted by John Dower in discussions with, in particular, Abercrombie, Spence and Symonds on behalf of FLD – and which were extensively used by CPRE in their negotiations with the Forestry Commission – helped to fix in the minds of government and public alike where the possible boundaries of the future Lake District National Park might be. This 'red line' map would be used in discussions once the CPRE Standing Committee for National Parks was set up, with a strong FLD representation, at the end of 1935.

At this point we can introduce the Reverend Henry Herbert Symonds (1885–1958). If Kenneth Spence was the key figure in the 1920s and early 1930s, and the main driving force behind the creation of FLD, Symonds was the main player who consolidated and carried FLD forward from the mid-1930s for nearly a quarter of a century until his death in 1958. The evidence of his FLD contemporaries, and the written records, is irrefutable. They confirm just how pivotal he was in establishing and maintaining FLD as a leading amenity group on the local and national stage.

Symonds was educated at Rugby school and Oxford University, and then followed a successful academic career in secondary education, during which he took religious orders, culminating as headmaster of the Liverpool Institute. He took early retirement in 1935 when he was 51 and moved to the Lake District from Liverpool. He then devoted himself more or less full-time, and unpaid, to FLD and the wider national park

15 Reverend H. H. Symonds (second from left) at Black Sail Hut, Ennerdale, 6 April 1934. From FLD archive, reproduced by kind permission of Friends of the Lake District.

cause. He was FLD's first treasurer, from 1934 until 1937; secretary from 1937 until 1948; chairman from 1948 until 1955; and vice president and hon. consultant from 1955 until his death. He took over from John Dower as hon. drafting secretary to the CPRE Standing Committee on National Parks in 1941, and was thence intimately involved with all the detailed campaigning work on behalf of CPRE and FLD for the establishment of national parks. Indeed his contemporaries regarded him as the main 'spear-carrier' for national parks from 1941 onwards, through his combined work with FLD and CPRE on behalf of all prospective national park areas. In 1937 he founded – with Theo Chorley – Lake District Farm Estates (see Chapter Four).

He was deeply knowledgeable about the Lake District,[1] and also developed a particular interest in, and knowledge of, Snowdonia, this from his days as headmaster at the Liverpool Institute. He was a self-confessed workaholic, a tenacious, erudite man who never took 'no' for an answer. Once he got his teeth into an issue or a campaign he would not let go until the outcome was determined. Crucially, he had a natural gift for paying attention to detailed facts and arguments as well as being able to articulate the bigger picture. It made no difference whether it was the government or its agencies, public authorities or private companies and landowners with whom he dealt. He would take on anybody and any organisation that posed a threat to the Lake District landscape (and after 1945 the threat to the heart of Snowdonia from a proposed hydro-electric scheme, which subsequently went ahead). In that respect he and Kenneth

Spence had much in common. Neither courted personal acclaim or popularity. As we will see, Symonds also carried the burden of the day-to-day work of FLD, and CPRE SCNP, virtually alone at a critical period through the 1939–1945 war years. In his outgoing FLD presidential address at the FLD AGM in 1969 Theo (now Lord) Chorley said, 'I suppose if one looks for the patron saint of the Friends, one comes back to Symonds'. Typically, in his entry for *Who Was Who 1951–1960*, Symonds describes his recreation as 'rescuing scraps of natural beauty'.[2]

Background to the dispute

The first large-scale blanket coniferous afforestation in the Lakes, some 2,000 acres, was carried out in 1908 by Manchester Corporation to secure the water catchment area of the Thirlmere reservoir (see Figure 2). This rigid and dense uniformity, with the significant reduction of public access and detrimental effects on flora and fauna, set the scene for future controversy.

In 1919 the Forestry Commission was established. Backed up by government funding, it was given the statutory duty to buy, through compulsory purchase if necessary, suitable land in England for large-scale afforestation, in order to secure a strategic reserve of home-grown timber in the face of any future supply threats from overseas, especially during any war. Although it had to have regard to public access and amenities, its primary purpose was to produce timber on a large scale, more or less as a cash crop. This inevitably meant reliance on fast-growing non-indigenous coniferous species, especially the Sitka spruce and larch. Early plantations had little or no regard to landscape morphology or history. They were large, and planted in densely packed geometric lines – taking advantage of existing enclosure boundary lines where appropriate. Concerns over the possible adverse landscape and ecological damage were very low on the list of priorities, but in making their purchases of land the Forestry Commission was keen to promote the 'forest park' concept. Therefore, they intended that some of the acreage would remain unplanted – where growth conditions were unfavourable. Further, parts of the newly-purchased Forestry Commission land would be opened up for public access, which had generally been denied on the hitherto privately-owned land. However, in the Lake District lack of existing public access to fell and dales was not an issue – a traditional *de facto* right to access existed, and much of the area was, in any case, common land. Therefore, it was argued that in the Lake District the introduction of a dense coniferous monoculture might actually diminish public access.

The first major Forestry Commission purchases in the Lake District were on the Thornthwaite Estate, near Whinlatter (1919) and in

FORESTRY COMMISSION

GRIZEDALE PIKE
CHRISTMAS TREES BELOW.   NATURAL BEAUTY BEYOND

Ennerdale, some 5,000 acres in 1925–1926. Mass coniferous afforestation took place at both locations in the late 1920s, although the Forestry Commission subsequently transferred over 3,500 acres of non-plantable high land around Ennerdale, including Great Gable and Pillar, to the National Trust. By the end of 1933 the Forestry Commission had planted nearly 1,250,000 larch and over 5,000,000 spruce trees in the Lake District.[3] The stage was then set for their next major purchase, but also for controversy.

16 Whinlatter: afforestation, early days. From FLD archive, reproduced by kind permission of Friends of the Lake District.

The 1934 Forestry Commission Purchase – Hardknott Forest Park and FLD's response

In October 1934, just as FLD was being formed, the Forestry Commission announced the purchase of a 7,240 acre estate in upper Eskdale and upper Dunnerdale. They subsequently indicated that the

7 Forestry
Commission at
Whinlatter. From
FLD archive,
reproduced by kind
permission of Friends
of the Lake District.

TREES ARCHITECTURE SHEDS AND SANITATION ALL BY THE FORESTRY COMMISSION

FORESTRY COMMISSION. WHINLATTER SMOTHERED BY COMMERCIAL SPRUCE

THE HEAD OF ENNERDALE. from *Scenery lyne*.

ENNERDALE HEAD
SAVED FROM THE FORESTRY COMMISSION

A47

18 Ennerdale Head saved. From FLD archive, reproduced by kind permission of Friends of the Lake District.

economically plantable area was some 2,100 acres, the remaining 5,000 acres being unplantable. The plantable area was to be the subject of great dispute.

From the outset FLD policy had two aims. Firstly, it would stand fast against any afforestation in Eskdale or Dunnerdale, but would also work out in detail (but in secret) which parts of the proposed plantable areas they would be prepared to negotiate about with the Forestry Commission, with reduction of the acreage in mind. Secondly, and as importantly, they would seek agreement from the Forestry Commission that a 'forest-free' exclusion zone should be established in as large an area as possible within the Lake District. From the outset, it was decided that FLD tactics to achieve these two aims would include, if necessary, the use of a public appeal as well as working behind the scenes with, and through, other amenity groups.

Opposition to the Forestry Commission amongst the amenity groups was far from uniform: initially the groups tended to act independently of each other. FLD's executive committee agreed that its first approach should be to try and buy the Forestry Commission out 'lock, stock and barrel'.[4] Symonds, on behalf of FLD, wrote to the Forestry Commission Chairman, Sir Roy Robinson, offering to buy back the whole of the Hardknott estate.[5] This offer was refused.

At the same time, the National Trust, through G. M. Trevelyan, was already negotiating with the Forestry Commission to see if some of the Lake District could be declared a 'forest free' zone. By January 1935 Trevelyan had secured an informal agreement for an exclusion zone to include Borrowdale, Newlands, the Langdales, and Eskdale head, while the Forestry Commission was prepared to consult before planting in Wasdale or between Ullswater and Windermere.[6]

In contrast, CPRE's stance was that it should negotiate with the Forestry Commission on a broader geographical basis than just the Lake District. As a national body it wanted to take a countrywide view on exclusion areas, negotiating with the Forestry Commission through 'give and take', not confrontation. This stance suited the Forestry Commission. Consequently, it was agreed to establish a joint informal Forestry Commission/CPRE Advisory Committee. The interests of the National Trust and the Commons, Open Spaces and Footpaths Preservation Society were represented under the CPRE umbrella. But, crucially, the Forestry Commission refused to negotiate directly with FLD. It felt, with some justice, that this would set a precedent for potentially protracted negotiations to take place with any amenity group throughout the country, wherever they intended to proceed with afforestation schemes.

At the first meeting of the joint advisory committee on 30 April 1935, it was minuted that CPRE 'might serve as the channel for complaints from local bodies and private individuals, e.g. the Friends of the Lake District', and that 'CPRE has called for a report from the Friends of the Lake District'.[7] The Forestry Commission had offered to reduce the plantable area by between 320 acres and 440 acres, subject to a £2 per acre compensation payment, and to plant more deciduous trees where soil conditions allowed. Herbert Griffin (CPRE secretary) wrote to Kenneth Spence (FLD secretary) enclosing the minutes of that first meeting. Spence, and the FLD chairman James Cropper, made it clear to Griffin that CPRE did not speak for FLD. The strength of FLD feeling against the Forestry Commission's proposals, and differences over tactics between FLD and CPRE at this time, are confirmed in a draft text for a letter, never sent, from Cropper to Sir Francis Acland, a member of the Forestry Commission (see Appendix 2). However, it was decided that FLD would prepare its report for submission by CPRE at the next joint meeting. It was also agreed that FLD should prepare to 'go public'. Tactics would now include raising a public petition as well as using contacts in Parliament and the press. Groundwork for the organisation of this petition got under way, as CPRE was informed when FLD sent them the report.

The threat of an active FLD public campaign went down badly with CPRE. However, the FLD Report, in which opposition to any afforestation in Eskdale/Dunnerdale was reiterated, was tabled by CPRE at the second joint meeting with the Forestry Commission on 28 May

PILLAR ROCK STILL VISIBLE 1937
FORESTRY COMMISSION

19 (*Left*) Ennerdale afforestation 1. From FLD archive, reproduced by kind permission of Friends of the Lake District.

20 (*Right*) Ennerdale afforestation 2. From FLD archive, reproduced by kind permission of Friends of the Lake District.

FORESTRY COMMISSION
SPRUCES CHOKING ENNERDALE

ENNERDALE.   THE END OF FREEDOM
FORESTRY   COMMISSION

FORESTRY   COMMISSION
N.W. SLOPES OF PILLAR FELL—LINE UPON LINE

1935. The Forestry Commission rejected CPRE/FLD proposals. CPRE felt that it was not in a strong negotiating position, and Herbert Griffin considered that any attempt by FLD 'to go public' would be counter-productive and only serve to harden the Forestry Commission position. CPRE was keen to prevent Lake District matters souring negotiations with the Forestry Commission in other potential national park areas, while the National Trust and Commons, Open Spaces and Footpaths Society felt that all-out opposition to afforestation in Eskdale/ Dunnerdale would jeopardise a wider exclusion zone in the Lakes and elsewhere.

Significantly, at the third joint Forestry Commission/CPRE meeting (12 July), John Dower's 'red line map', showing a proposed forest exclusion zone for the Lakes, was tabled by CPRE. The Forestry Commission was in favour of negotiating a Lake District 'exclusion zone' but did not move on its earlier concessions regarding reductions in plantable land in Eskdale and Dunnerdale. CPRE, with National Trust and Commons, Open Spaces and Footpaths Society acquiescence, decided to accept these terms. A press release to this effect was put out in August 1935. FLD, forewarned, then carried out their threat to launch their public petition, which they did in mid-October 1935. It had over 12,000 signatures, including a large part of the British church, legal, academic and political establishment.[8]

FLD/CPRE relations, in particular between the two secretaries, Kenneth Spence and Herbert Griffin, deteriorated further. Griffin resigned from FLD's executive committee, citing his busy commitments as secretary of CPRE. Symonds, in turn, resigned from the recently-established Lancashire branch of CPRE. Spence was ousted as secretary of the Lake District Safeguarding Society (LDSS) after suggesting that FLD and LDSS should consider merging. This debate subsequently led to James Cropper resigning as chairman of FLD in 1937, in favour of retaining his chairmanship of LDSS. He waited until the afforestation issue was resolved because he endorsed FLD's stance, but wanted LDSS to continue as an independent amenity group, rather than merging with FLD. He remained a member of FLD's executive committee. Within CPRE ranks, Abercrombie disagreed with Griffin over the lack of support for FLD in negotiations with the Forestry Commission: 'For the first time in 10 years we have not seen eye to eye over this wretched Eskdale affair'.[9] Further evidence of residual differences of approach between FLD and CPRE comes in a postscript of a letter written by Herbert Griffin to Geoffrey Mander M.P. dated 27 November 1937:

> Have you seen H. H. Symonds' book entitled "Afforestation in the Lake District" published by Dent yesterday? I have not read it, but knowing Symonds I suspect it is very violent – probably too violent for

me! It has references to the Lake District as a National Park and the absence of a national policy on pp 14–16, 66–69, 71–73, and 75–78.[10]

The FLD petition and public campaign had no effect on securing further concessions from the Forestry Commission in its proposed Hardknott Forest Park, but it did influence later Forestry Commission/CPRE negotiations over afforestation policy generally in the Lake District. Their fourth joint meeting took place on 3 March 1936. But now the Forestry Commission was in an even stronger bargaining position, for the Government saw afforestation as one way of dealing with the huge unemployment problem. The Forestry Commission budget was increased and funds were earmarked for new afforestation projects within 15 miles of all the Special Areas in the country.[11] Since much of the potential Lake District national park area was within 15 miles of the West Cumberland Special Area boundary the heightened threat was obvious.

Many people, the FLD executive committee included, did not think that this new measure would lead to any significant extra jobs in afforestation. Symonds, in particular, countered the case for employment relief from new afforestation in chapter four of his book *Afforestation in the Lake District*. To their credit, the Forestry Commission Commissioners indicated, in spite of their new powers, that in respect of the Lake District they were still prepared to negotiate a self-imposed 'exclusion zone'. Dower's FLD 'red line' map, tabled by CPRE, ring-fenced some 520 square miles. The Forestry Commission countered that it would refrain from new planting within an area of 220–240 square miles; they would also have regard to the red line boundaries as long as they could purchase suitable land outside it. CPRE recommended acceptance of these new terms.

FLD continued with what might be termed its high-risk strategy by rejecting them, and triggering a debate in the House of Lords on afforestation. By this time FLD's campaign had certainly caught the ear of Government, if not necessarily favourably. At prime minister's question time on 11 February 1936, the Labour MP Geoffrey Mander asked Baldwin whether he was aware of the Lake District afforestation 'problem'. Baldwin replied that he was but the Forestry Commissioners had assured him that due consideration was being given to 'amenity' in their plans. Mander then asked 'Is the Prime Minister aware that another important body, 'The Friends of the Lake District', are still very far from being satisfied with the arrangements?' Baldwin's reply was 'I doubt whether they will ever be satisfied. I think the work of the [Forestry Commission/CPRE] Co-ordinating Committee has done a deal of good and will do more'.[12]

The threat of the Lord's debate led the Forestry Commission and CPRE to convene an emergency meeting on 18 March, to see if further

CONIFERS FOR ESKDALE

FORESTRY COMMISSION

NOW NOT TO BE PLANTED.   COMPENSATION TO BE PAID BY THE PUBLIC

21 Eskdale saved 1.
From FLD archive,
reproduced by kind
permission of Friends
of the Lake District.

22 Eskdale saved 2.
From FLD archive,
reproduced by kind
permission of Friends
of the Lake District.

concessions could be made. By this time Kenneth Spence had joined the executive of Commons, Open Spaces and Footpaths Society and convinced them to stand out for better terms. The National Trust shared CPRE's view that the Forestry Commission terms were reasonable. During the debate, on 1 April 1936, Lord Crawford, CPRE President, spoke against the motion and for the Forestry Commission. Although the outcome was inconclusive it did gain national publicity. As a result the Forestry Commission agreed to meet an FLD delegation on 16 June. By then FLD had reduced its 'red line' area from 520 to 420 square miles, and the Forestry Commission added the southern slopes of Skiddaw, Loweswater, and an addition north of Ullswater, Martindale, and Troutbeck to its self-imposed excluded areas. At the meeting FLD further reduced its 'red line' area to 390 square miles and the Forestry Commission raised theirs to 275 square miles. By then the areas where controversy remained were Kentmere, Esthwaite, Coniston, and Eskdale/Dunnerdale.

In July 1936 the Forestry Commission agreed a 'red line' area covering 300 square miles of the Lake District, and both FLD and CPRE decided that negotiations with the Forestry Commission had run their course and should be concluded. The southern part of the Lake District was still in dispute and unprotected from afforestation, but the Forestry Commission stated that – in acquiring and planting properties bought in this area – they would have regard to 'amenity' (see Map 2).

The 1936 Forestry Commission/Council for the Preservation of Rural England Agreement

From its own perspective FLD had thus secured, through its forceful and tenacious campaigning tactics, significant concessions, from the Forestry Commission. The threat of large-scale state coniferous afforestation in the central core of the future national park area had receded. The Government issued a White Paper giving full details of the agreement between the Forestry Commission and CPRE in July 1936 (there is no reference in the paper to FLD),[13] and this might have ended the matter. But not for FLD, which was still deeply concerned about future Forestry Commission plans in the Lake District outside the new central exclusion zone, and especially for those 'areas subject to special considerations' agreed on the map included in the White Paper. This meant that large parts of Eskdale and Dunnerdale as well as land between Coniston Water and Windermere remained targets for large-scale coniferous afforestation, together with other parts of the Lake District (as was borne out by subsequent Forestry Commission purchases).

It was at this stage that Symonds' book *Afforestation in the Lake District* was published, with the Foreword written by FLD President Lord Howard of Penrith. It was an account (from FLD's point of view) of the

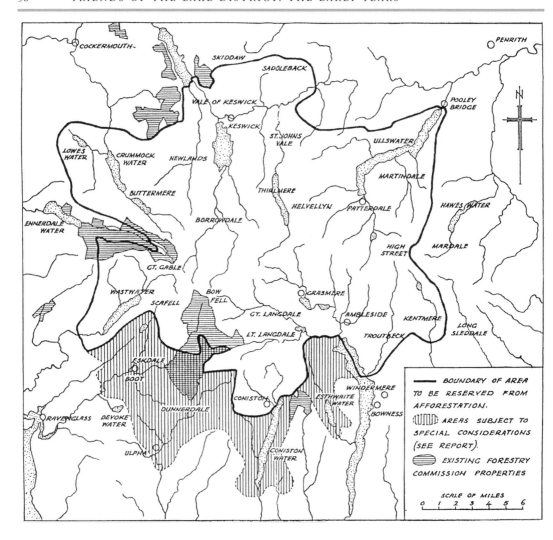

progress of the Forestry Commission/CPRE negotiations over the proposed Hardknott Forest Park, and a detailed riposte to the rationale behind the Forestry Commission policy of large-scale coniferous afforestation in the Lake District to date.[14] Symonds undoubtedly merely expressed, albeit in his own inimitable style, what was clearly the consistent policy of FLD during this protracted 'quarrel'. Furthermore, FLD now considered strategies to counter further Forestry Commission activities in those 'sensitive areas', deemed 'at risk', outside the central Lake District exclusion zone. One short-term tactic was to commission a detailed technical report on the background to, and progress of, the large mid-1920s Ennerdale land purchase.[15] Although the report made a detailed case against the Forestry Commission it was never made public, but it added at least one professional forestry viewpoint[16] to strengthen and add credibility to the FLD case in future disagreements with

MAP 2 Forestry Commission afforestation exclusion zone 'red line map'. 1936 CPRE/FC White Paper. From FLD archive, reproduced by kind permission of Friends of the Lake District.

CONIFERS FOR DUNNERDALE

FORESTRY COMMISSION
ACROSS BIRKS BRIDGE.   TO BE PLANTED OUT

the Forestry Commission. The other strategy, with longer term consequences, was to consider entering the land purchase and ownership market; specifically, to buy farms in areas deemed 'sensitive' and under threat, to prevent their purchase by the Forestry Commission, or to delay matters if the Forestry Commission proceeded to apply for compulsory purchase orders. This would also prevent purchase for speculative residential property development, a concern of FLD (and other amenity groups such as the National Trust) in the mid-1930s. The direct result of these deliberations was the formation of the Lake District Farm Estates company (see Chapter Four).

As a result of the 1936 Forestry Commission/CPRE Joint Agreement the Commission agreed to exclude planting in Upper Eskdale altogether in exchange of compensation at the rate of

23 Conifers for Dunnerdale 1. From FLD archive, reproduced by kind permission of Friends of the Lake District.

CONIFERS FOR DUNNERDALE

FORESTRY COMMISSION
BACKGROUND TO BE PLANTED TO 1500 FEET

24 Conifers for Dunnerdale 2. From FLD archive, reproduced by kind permission of Friends of the Lake District.

£2 per acre. A public appeal was subsequently made by CPRE, the National Trust and Commons, Open Spaces and Footpaths Society to raise the £1,480 required to compensate the Forestry Commission. The first two contributions were from Prof. G. M. Trevelyan (£50) and FLD (£25) and the fund was oversubscribed. However, the Forestry Commission and the National Trust, in the eyes of FLD, then dragged their feet in agreeing the formal restrictive covenants. Both parties were content with an exchange of letters as the basis for the agreement, and after the outbreak of the Second World War, the National Trust stance was that resolution should wait until after the cessation of hostilities. FLD disagreed and pushed for a formalisation of the agreement, pointing out that the Eskdale Appeal had been carried out on that basis. Therefore, the issue of restrictive covenants would remain on the agenda into the 1940s.[17]

Notes

[1]   Symonds' book *Walking in the Lake District* remains one of the best walking and descriptive guides to the Lakes.

[2]   Symonds was also actively involved in other amenity groups. He was vice president (1935–1952) and then president (1953–1956) of the Ramblers' Association, and a pioneer of the youth hostel movement in this country, establishing the very first youth hostels, in Snowdonia, and was then founder and vice president of the Merseyside YHA.

[3]   See Forestry Commission *14th Annual Report*, 1933.

[4]   The matter was first discussed by the executive committee at its second meeting held on 2 January 1936, in Windermere, when 'Mr Symonds asked that he might be instructed to make enquiries at the Forestry Commission concerning the proposals for Eskdale and other parts of the Lake District and the Secretary was asked to give him written authority to do this'.

[5]   Letter from H. H. Symonds to Sir R. Robinson, 15 February 1935. CRO (Kendal) WDSO/117/VI/1/2.

[6]   See Symonds notes of 2 October : CRO (Kendal) WDSO/117/VI/1/2.

[7]   CPRE Monthly Report, June 1935, p. 22.

[8]   See H. H. Symonds, *Afforestation in the Lake District*, Appendix 1 for the names of the main establishment petitioners.

[9]   File SR CPRE C/1/89/19 (formerly 181/1).

[10] See CPRE SR/1/102/10.

[11] This was the Special Areas Afforestation Scheme.

[12] See *The Manchester Guardian*, 12 February 1936.

[13] *Afforestation in the Lake District – A Report by the Joint Informal Committee of the Forestry Commission and the Council for the Preservation of Rural England.* HMSO, 1936.

[14] The following extract was recorded in the FLD Minutes, 23 August 1937:
      'The Hon. Treasurer [Symonds] offered a large number of copies of his book on the subject for free distribution, provided the Society would pay for the cost of postage.

He was warmly thanked for his offer which was accepted. The terms were agreed of a slip to be printed and enclosed (together with one of the Society's membership forms) inviting acceptance of the book'.

[15]   For an interesting and fuller account of the report on the Forestry Commission's Ennerdale land purchase (and another account of aspects of the afforestation dispute during the 1930s), see L. M. Mullett, '"The blast of a fog-horn during the performance of a Brahm's symphony": afforestation in the Lake District and its role in the Friends of the Lake District conservation movement of the 1930s', Unpublished Diploma dissertation, Lancaster University, 2007.

[16]   The author was William Bennett, a forester and chairman of the Royal English Forestry Society. See Mullett, pp. 23–27.

[17]   Although a 'gentleman's agreement' it was always subsequently adhered to by all parties. And after the National Park Authority was established in 1951 it always regarded it as an indispensable backstop and was always given prominence in national park plans. For example, para 3.12 (p. 53) of the 1978 National Park Plan states 'In the absence of planning control over afforestation, the 1936 Agreement limiting Forestry Commission acquisitions has provided the basis of the Planning Board's policies on afforestation and has given rise to the presumption that any planting of bare land, of whatever scale, should take place outside the 'central area'.

THE CHIEF LOCAL INDUSTRY

25 'Traditional sheep farming'. From FLD archive, reproduced by kind permission of Friends of the Lake District.

ESKDALE SHOW.   THEN WINTER

CHAPTER FOUR

Lake District Farm Estates: 1937–1977[1]

Well, let's do it.

Symonds to Chorley. From 'Origins and History of Lake District Farm
Estates Company', Lord Chorley, 1974.

Once FLD had formally agreed to pursue the farm purchase and
management option, the detailed planning and preparation were largely
undertaken by Symonds and Chorley (see previous chapter). Robert
Samuel Theodore Chorley (Theo) (1895–1978) was born in Kendal. He
attended Kendal School and Queen's College, Oxford, where he studied
law. He was an enthusiastic rock climber in his youth, and very active in
the Fell and Rock Climbing Club. He was called to the bar in 1920, but
went on to have an outstanding university academic career in law. At the
time that Lake District Farm Estates (LDFE) was established, Chorley
was vice-chairman of the National Trust, hon. secretary of CPRE,
president of FRCC, as well as being a member of FLD. He was Professor
of Commercial and Industrial Law in the University of London. Chorley
and Symonds were friends. Chorley had helped secure the National Trust
Act 1937. This gave the National Trust important new legal powers to
hold restrictive covenants over land and property as if it were its own
planning authority (see below for its significance for LDFE). In spite of
subsequently taking on other leading roles in the academic and political
worlds, as well as various conservation and outdoor societies, he
continued to take an active interest in LDFE until it was wound up in
1977. Among his other roles he was vice-president of FLD from 1946 to
1960 and joint vice-president from 1969 until 1978, president of the
Holiday Fellowship 1947–1957, president of the British Mountaineering
Council 1950–1953, vice-president of the Alpine Club 1956–1958, and
president of the Commons Open Spaces and Footpaths Preservation
Society 1961–1975. His son, the current Lord Chorley, is a vice-president
of FLD.

In March 1974, in an article 'Origins and History of Lake District
Farm Estates Company',[2] Chorley confirmed that he and Symonds had,
over a seven-year period, worked together on 'matters affecting the Lake

26 R. S. T. Chorley, President of the Fell and Rock Climbing Club of the English Lake District, 1935–1937. Reproduced from the The Journal of the Fell and Rock Climbing Club of the English Lake District, Vol. X (No. 2), 1935, by kind permission of the FRCC.

District'. He went on to say they had 'just come through a particularly anxious period during which we had been fighting off the encroachments of the Forestry Commission in central Lakeland'. However, it was the 1936 public sale of the Robinson estate in Langdale which finally led to the idea of establishing LDFE: the estate was being marketed nationwide as being ideal for second or holiday homes. Chorley made it clear that the stretched financial position of the National Trust meant that it could not bid at the sale, but portions of the estate were purchased by 'well-to-do' friends, including Mrs Heelis, better known as Beatrix Potter;

restrictive covenants were thence agreed with them and the National Trust to preserve their use as dales farms. Crucially, he goes on to say:

> an unforeseen result of our efforts however was a number of offers to subscribe to the raising of a fund from which a purchase could be made. Time was too short and organisation was absent, so nothing could be done on those lines. But discussing the campaign in retrospect I remarked to Symonds that if we could have issued and sold shares in a property company we could have bought in at any rate on one of the Robinson farms. To which he replied in his typically forthright way, 'well let's do it'.[3]

27 Lake District Farm Estates. 1937 pamphlet front cover – Skelwith farm, Brathay valley. From FLD archive, reproduced by kind permission of Friends of the Lake District.

A letter sent from Symonds to Chorley dated 26 January 1937, in which he comments on Chorley's first draft of a 'Proposal to Form Lake District Farm Estates Limited', is a key document here.[4] It shows what might be called the 'typical' Symonds style; demonstrates the informal, friendly relationships between the two men, who obviously liked and respected each other, and confirms the view that the piecemeal sale of farms to 'off-comers' for second homes and the Forestry Commission's active farm purchase policy were the two driving forces behind the idea for LDFE. It also highlights that the National Trust at the time had neither the organisation nor the funds to be an active player in the farm purchase market: rather it relied on gifts or covenants. Indeed, it was still not a major landowner in the Lake District, and would not be so until well after the Second World War. For example, in 1945 the National Trust owned 31 farms, 17,000 acres of land and 74 other houses and cottages, and 17,000 acres in the Lake District protected by covenants. This represented about three per cent of the Lake District and put its holdings below those of the Forestry Commission, Manchester Corporation Waterworks Department and several private landowners.[5]

Thus LDFE's purpose was to purchase, own and manage land and buildings in the Lake District, the area to be as defined by the Addison Committee on National Parks, 1931,

LAKE DISTRICT FARM ESTATES
LIMITED

SKELWITH FARM, BRATHAY VALLEY

Registered Office,
Exchange Chambers,
Kendal

28 Rannerdale farm, Crummock Water. From FLD archive, reproduced by kind permission of Friends of the Lake District.

29 High Wallabarrow farm, Duddon Valley. From FLD archive, reproduced by kind permission of Friends of the Lake District.

and to maintain them in their current use. The rules of the company stated that upon a LDFE purchase the farm and its land would be placed under a restrictive National Trust covenant. This was an immediate and direct benefit resulting from Chorley's success in getting new legal powers under the National Trust Act, 1937. The National Trust could now hold restrictive covenants on its own properties, or those of other owners placed under covenant with them. It meant that although the Forestry Commission could use compulsory purchase orders in acquiring land, any subsequent proposed change of use to forestry from farming would, if it was held under National Trust covenant, require primary legislation in Parliament on each occasion and for each proposed purchase – a very time-consuming process and almost impossible to achieve. The same legal covenanting applied, and still applies, to all properties gifted or leased to or purchased outright by the National Trust, and is a very powerful weapon in their armoury. As an extra safeguard the rules of the new company required that the National Trust would have first refusal on any subsequent offer for sale of a LDFE property.

LDFE was financed largely from purchases of shares in the company by FLD members. Each shareholder could only purchase shares to a maximum value of £200. The start-up capital was £6,935, spread among 48 shareholders (well below the desired level of £50,000 for the purchase of 25 farms at an estimated market value of £2,000 each). Symonds was vice-chairman and Chorley was on the management committee, which also had representatives from CPRE, FLD and the National Trust. The company employed a professional land agent to manage the 17 farms which it purchased during its forty-year lifetime. It was successful in concentrating its purchases in the early days in 'sensitive' areas just outside the voluntary central exclusion zone established under the 1936 Joint Forestry Commission/CPRE Agreement on Afforestation. Areas deemed particularly vulnerable included the Duddon Valley, Eskdale, lower Wasdale, lower Langdale, and Longsleddale. However, one of the first purchases (in 1938) was Rannerdale Farm, Crummock Water, specifically to protect the road to and from Buttermere from any 'improvement' and to fill a gap in National Trust protection of the lake area (see Figure 28).

By 1948, eleven farms had been purchased (see Table 1). Prices paid depended, of course, on size and location, but varied from £1,350, for Harrowhead Farm (1948), to £3,800, for Skelwith Fold Farm (1938). Each farm was purchased on economic grounds, to earn a return, as well as for agricultural use and landscape protection.

However, LDFE increasingly struggled to raise adequate further capital (especially via FLD members buying LDFE shares) to purchase more properties. The company remained relatively under-capitalised: the £50,000 initial start-up capital proposed when the company was set up in 1937 had still not been achieved by the 1960s. Moreover, land values increased considerably during the post-war period. Indeed, in Theo Chorley's first report as the new Chairman of LDFE, in 1946, he stated that the 'capital cost at which farms, even in the Lake District, today change hands is out of proportion even to the moderate return for which the company looks, and this is making it difficult to enlarge the company's holdings in ways which are financially sound'.[6] The twin problems of relative under-capitalisation and increases in farm property prices caused some management committee members to question the validity of continuing to offer the National Trust first option to buy an LDFE farm if it was up for sale, when it could well fetch a higher price on the open market.[7]

This led to a long and sometimes acrimonious internal debate about the future of LDFE and its *raison d'etre*. During the period from 1955 to 1970 only six more farms were purchased (see Table 1). Matters came to a head in 1973 with the proposed sale of High Wallawbarrow Farm, the first farm bought by LDFE in 1938 (see Figure 29). Initially, a resolution was passed by a narrow majority of the LDFE management committee to hold a public auction for its sale, with the caveat that a National Trust covenant be included in the legal arrangements for its purchase. FLD raise strong objections, and Chorley (now president of LDFE) proposed an injunction to stop the public auction.[8] The management committee then agreed to end the sale of High Wallawbarrow Farm by public auction, and instead to put the property out to tender. Although not the highest bidder, the National Trust's tender price of £20,000 was accepted.

A lengthy debate at the 1974 AGM was informed by Chorley and his article 'Origins and History of Lake District Farm Estates', and was held in the light of the dispute over the sale of High Wallawbarrow Farm. Eventually it was agreed that the time was ripe for reviewing the future of LDFE.

Accordingly, in March 1975 Chorley published a paper 'The Future of the Society'.[9] In it he confirmed and reiterated that 'the financial stringency' of the 1930s had prevented the National Trust from being more active in outright land purchases, leading to the idea for LDFE. Therefore 'the Founders had a basic purpose to act as a long stop for the Trust, and in no sense as a rival organisation'. It 'hoped to buy properties which the Trust could not afford to buy'. It was appropriate and timely to review the future of LDFE. Having weighed up the 'pros' and 'cons', and stating that the 'status quo' was a viable option, he nevertheless strongly recommended that negotiations should take place with the National Trust with the purpose of handing the current portfolio of farms over to them, and then winding up the company. The National Trust had now become the largest single landowner in the Lake District. It also had a much larger financial base than LDFE and considerable expertise in farm management. The afforestation 'threat' was much diminished, for Forestry Commission policy was now changing from acquiring new land for large-scale mainly coniferous plantations to managing its existing ones. It was also gradually changing its emphasis from a dense and uniform coniferous monoculture to a more mixed deciduous forestry regime. Furthermore, the National Park now existed, with planning powers that afforded greater, if not complete, landscape protection.

Therefore, Chorley was of the view that LDFE should be wound up. After much, and sometimes fraught, internal debate this policy was agreed.

The company was formally wound up in 1977: the remaining ten farms that it owned were gifted to the National Trust. Symbolically, and fittingly, Chorley who helped, with Symonds, to set up the company was present, in his role as president of LDFE, at the handing over ceremony held at Yew Tree Farm, Rosthwaite, Borrowdale on 17 June 1977 (see Figure 30).

TABLE 1: Farms purchased over the lifetime of LDFE 1937–1977

	Bought	Gifted/Sold	Name	Acreage
1	1938	1974 (NT)	*High Wallawbarrow Farm* Duddon Valley	127
2	1938	1954 (Tenant)	*Rannerdale Farm* Crummock Water	48
3	1938	1955 (Tenant)	*Skelwith Fold Farm* Ambleside	439
4	1941	1958 (NT)	*Low Wallawbarrow Farm & Pannelholme Intakes* Duddon Valley	252
5	1941	1977 (NT)*	*Mireside Farm* Ennerdale	495
6,7,8	1943	1977 (NT)*	*Buckbarrow, Broad Gap & Gill Farms* Wasdale	255
9	1944	1944 (NT)	*Stockdale Farm* Longsleddale	318
10	1948	1968 (NT)	*Longhouse Farm* Dunnderdale	
11	1948	1977 (NT)*	*Harrowhead Farm* Nether Wasdale	86
12	1955	1977 (NT)*	*Gill Bank Farm* Boot, Eskdale	87
13	1956	1977 (NT)*	*How Green Farm* Hartsop, Ullswater	509
14	1956/7	1960 (NT)	*Biggard Mire Farm* Duddon Valley	254
15	1956/7	1977 (NT)*	*Yew Tree Farm* Borrowdale	582 (part)
16	1963	1977 (NT)*	*Longthwaite Farm* Borrowdale	582 (part)
17	1970	1977 (NT)*	*High Nook Farm* Loweswater	365

* Gifted to the NT on the winding up of LDFE in 1977

Notes

30 Handing-over ceremony LDFE farms to the National Trust, Yew Tree Farm, Borrowdale, 17 June 1977. Left to right: Lord Chorley, LDFE President, Mark Norman, NT Deputy Chairman. Reproduced by permission of the National Trust.

1   For a fuller study of LDFE see J. H. Cousins, 'Lake District Farm Estates Ltd – a History: 1937–1977', Diploma dissertation, University of Lancaster, 2000 (Copy also held at FLD HQ.); See relevant archives in CRO (Kendal), Lake District Farms Estates Ltd, WDSO 117, Section B, VI, 105/1.

2   Cousins, p. 8.

3   Ibid, p. 8.

4   Cousins, Appendix One, p. 28.

5   See Battrick p. vi.

6   Cousins, p. 17.

7   Interestingly, Symonds owned in his own name four farms. It is not established when he bought them, but it can be reasonably assumed that it was in the mid-1930s. Three were in Dunnerdale, just outside the Forestry Commission 'exclusion' zone, and one was in Borrowdale; all were in 'sensitive' areas, so it can be assumed that he bought them to retain their use as sheep farms and to protect their future against purchase by 'offcomers', or the Forestry Commission. He gifted all four to the National Trust in 1950, suggesting his complete confidence in their ability to secure their future as sheep farms. The three Dunnerdale farms were Hazel Head (242 acres), Pike Side Farm and Beckstones (255 acres) and Browside and Thrang Farms (170 acres); the other one was Banks Intake, Borrowdale (186 acres); Cousins p. 18, footnote 51.

[8] FLD's view was that if a LDFE property was sold it was not always necessary to get the best possible open market price. See Cousins p. 21, footnote 61.

[9] Cousins, Appendix Ten, pp. 45–51.

CRUMMOCK WATER & WHITELESS PIKE

31 Crummock Water and Whiteless Pike. From FLD archive, reproduced by kind permission of Friends of the Lake District.

CHAPTER FIVE

Roads, electricity and other stories: 1934–1939

> *We are against 'improvement' of the by-roads and mountain trackways in the Lake District. Motorists get more than they ask, and walkers lose what they need. Leave the passes for walkers. Leave the by-roads untarred. Leave the grass verges. No more grants from the Ministry of Transport, no increase of county rates to 'open up' this district. Leave well alone.*

> FLD Pamphlet, *A Road Policy for the Lake District* (1938).

Two of the other major issues that FLD had to come to terms with during the 1930s were the increasing number of motor vehicles on the roads (with the consequent pressure to 'improve' them, to respond to this greater traffic volume) and the spread of the benefits of electricity, and telephones, throughout the Lake District and wider Cumbrian region (with the issue of its visual impact on the landscape). FLD's responses to these two sets of developments are covered below.

The motor transport revolution and Lake District tracks and roads

The coming of motor transport in the twentieth century was an even more radical transport revolution than that of the railway in the nineteenth century. Cars, motor coaches, buses and lorries could now in theory go anywhere where there were suitable roads. And where existing roads and tracks were unsuitable there was pressure to 'improve' them. Thus controversy about roads, proposed new routes and improved existing ones, around and within the Lake District was bound to occur.

Early disputes focused on various proposals for improving road access within the dales and over the mountain passes (where necessary by creating minor roads from unimproved tracks). In addition, proposed improvements to the main through route from Kendal, via Windermere, Ambleside, and Grasmere, to Keswick were questioned, as were proposals for a Keswick bypass. Some minor road proposals will be considered first, then some of those for the major routes.

An examination of a relief map of the Lake District makes it clear there is really only one possible north-south route through the centre –

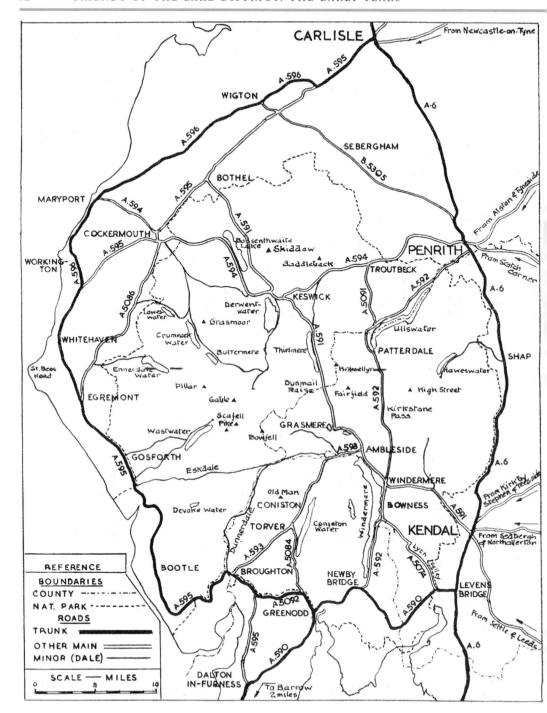

MAP 3 Sketch map of Cumbrian roads from FLD pamphlet *A Road Policy for the Lake District*, 1938. From FLD archive, reproduced by kind permission of Friends of the Lake District.

A ROAD POLICY
FOR THE
LAKE DISTRICT

Is THIS your policy ?

Issued by the FRIENDS OF THE LAKE DISTRICT,
AMBLESIDE.

32 Traffic congestion 1930s style. Cover from *A Road Policy for the Lake District*, FLD, 1938. From FLD archive, reproduced by kind permission of Friends of the Lake District.

that from Keswick over the wide, relatively low, pass of Dunmail Raise, via Ambleside to Kendal (the current A591). There is a route from Penrith past Ullswater and over the Kirkstone Pass to Troutbeck (the current A592) but this follows much more difficult terrain. There are no easy east-west routes since the central mountain core has to be traversed. The road from Ambleside up Little Langdale over Wrynose and Hardknott Passes and down Eskdale to the coast at Ravenglass was, and is, difficult. The situation in the Lake District contrasts with, for example, Snowdonia, where relief and topography have combined to allow more major routes to cut through and across the national park. To the north the route from Penrith to the west coast via Keswick and Cockermouth (the present A66, but original unimproved A594) follows easier terrain. In the south the route to the west coast (the present A590) meanders around Morecambe Bay mostly outside the Lake District. To the east, the England-Scotland route (the present A6) from Kendal to Penrith goes via Shap summit. Thus it was predictable that controversy would occur with proposals to improve these four main routes as well as the many unimproved rural minor tracks and roads. And controversy there was – and still is today.

It has to be said that FLD were not wholly successful during the 1930s in achieving the aim of 'leaving well alone'. The views of FLD were at variance with those of the three Lake District highways authorities, especially that of Cumberland County Council. In fact as early as August 1934, just before FLD was launched, Cumberland proposed to the Government's Commissioner for the Special Area of West Cumberland a series of minor road schemes that involved the tarmacing of previously unimproved tracks and improving (i.e. straightening and widening) existing minor roads: Styhead was included at a cost of £16,500; Wrynose and Hardknott, £12,000 for the four miles that were in Cumberland; Duddon Bridge, by Buck Barrow and Corney Fell to Waberthwaite, £22,500; Duddon Bridge by the 'Traveller's Rest' and Birker Moor to

THE ENNERDALE TRACKWAY
WHAT DO YOU WANT MORE?

33 Mountain access: foot or car? From FLD archive, reproduced by kind permission of Friends of the Lake District.

HARDKNOTT BEING SPOILED. CUMB^D C.C.
CURVE BANKED & EASED FOR UNWANTED CARS

Eskdale Green, £27,000; and Seatoller by Honister Hause to Buttermere, £6,000. Cumberland County Council gave four reasons for these schemes: they would stimulate trade by reducing the mileage travelled; provide employment while the work was undertaken; bring more visitors and improve the hotel trade; and open up a unique countryside that was, it was argued, 'gradually being forgotten owing to present inaccessibility'.[1] However, of these five schemes, only the Honister one went ahead in full. An amended Birker Moor scheme was also implemented. The failure of the other three was more for economic reasons than because of opposition from FLD and others, and a 5,000 signature FLD protest petition. The Honister road was funded by an *ad hoc* grant from the Ministry of Transport (see Figure 36). Undaunted, in 1936 Cumberland County Council proposed a scheme to tarmac and widen the rural mountain track through Newlands valley over Newlands Hause to Buttermere, and this went ahead in 1937 (see Figure 35).

As already stated, the major north/south through road in the Lake District was always the subject of controversy when improvement schemes were put forward. However, it should be emphasised that pressures for change were coloured by the traffic circumstances of the 1930s, when the huge growth in private car ownership had not yet taken place. Rather this was the period when commercial lorries and passenger motor coaches dominated the roads. Even so, private car ownership, although low by post-1945 standards, doubled between 1930 and 1939, from approximately one to two million.[2] On the A6, the main trunk route on the west side of

NEWLANDS ROAD. CUMBERLAND C.C.

WIDENED AND BLASTED 1937

AS IT WAS IN 1935

the country between England and Scotland, the section over the Shap Fells and across the high country around Shap village (at over 1,000 feet) was notoriously difficult: it was often closed for extended periods, especially during the winter, and it had not yet been much improved (see Figure 37). Consequently, lorries often used the A591 through the central Lake District as an alternative 'low level' route between England and Scotland, as did those heading to and from Maryport, Whitehaven, Workington and other west Cumberland towns via the A591 or the 'unimproved' A594 to Penrith and the A6. There was, of course, no M6 motorway. Therefore, from an early date FLD had a 'twin track' policy. They objected to attempts to make the A591 a major trunk route whilst at the same time lobbying for major improvements to the A6 to the east and the present A590 to the south and west of the Lake District. Indeed at the very first executive committee meeting in October 1934:

> The questioning of the widening of the Ambleside-Keswick road was referred to. The Secretary was instructed to write the AA and RAC with a view to obtaining their support regarding the undesirability of using this road as an alternative through route to Scotland, and to the County Council suggesting that steady improvements be carried out on the Shap Road, especially in the Borrow Bridge area (see Figure 38).

Later in the 1930s, FLD even commissioned a detailed feasibility study into the possible re-routing of a section of the A6 to avoid Shap Summit: this involved taking it through the lower ground of the Lune Valley south

35 Widening of Newlands road, 1937. From FLD archive, reproduced by kind permission of Friends of the Lake District.

THE RUIN OF HONISTER

THE ABOMINATION OF DESOLATION

ALL THE FUN

WALKING SPOILED

FULL SPEED FOR QUIET BUTTERMERE

B27

6 Honister tarmaced, 1935/6. From FLD archive, reproduced by kind permission of Friends of the Lake District.

of Tebay, on the line of the present M6. One other suggestion was to make a new line for the A6 from Lancaster along the entire Lune valley to Tebay. However, in spite of FLD objections, Cumberland County Council went ahead with a programme of road widening and straightening on the A591 from Thirlmere to the outskirts of Keswick – the results of which are evident today. Westmorland County Council did not, during this period, make any serious attempt to alter its section of the A591, from Kendal to Grasmere and thence to Dunmail Raise. However, it did propose, without proceeding any further than the initial planning stage, the first of many schemes for a bypass at Ambleside. In 1939, FLD supported Keswick Urban District Council in successfully opposing a Cumberland County Council proposal for a southern bypass of Keswick. Part of the proposed alignment would have taken it through Crow Park near Derwentwater, and the southern bypass scheme never re-emerged. However, at that time FLD would not have opposed a bypass to the north of the town, albeit a single carriageway with suitable landscaping.

Work also proceeded during the 1930s on minor road works which involved introducing a more 'urban' style of road design and maintenance into rural areas. This might involve widening a carriageway here and there, ironing out small bends and introducing road markings and signage. The unique character of these rural highways and byways was not yet thought to be of sufficient importance to merit protection as important historic features in a fragile landscape. Improved access, and traffic flow were the priorities, often in the name of better road safety. This was an official mindset that FLD sought to challenge and change. Challenge FLD continued to do; change was harder to achieve.

The inevitable consequence of the tarmacing of previously unimproved tracks (such as, for example, Honister and Newlands passes and routes in Dunnerdale) was that access by private motor vehicles was possible for the first time (though not for public motor coaches). Previously, access to most dales, daleheads and mountain passes was only possible by foot and, in some cases, horse. Relatively limited private car ownership during the 1930s and 1940s somewhat restricted the environmental and human impact at this time. And of course some parts of the Lake District are, even today, relatively inaccessible, even with tarmaced road surfaces, simply because of the rugged terrain of the area.

37 Shap Fell in Winter, 1938. From FLD archive, reproduced by kind permission of Friends of the Lake District.

HUCK BROW, SHAP
THE WORST STRETCH ON A6

RADICAL IMPROVEMENT OF A6
WILL PROTECT THE LAKE DISTRICT

38 Hucks Brow, A6.
From FLD archive,
reproduced by kind
permission of Friends
of the Lake District.

For example, although the only east-west minor road, from Ambleside to Ravenglass via Little Langdale, Wrynose, Hardknott and Eskdale, was tarmaced along its entire length after 1945, it is still narrow and difficult to navigate. However, with the vast increase in car ownership from 1960 onwards there was inevitably increased visitor pressure and impact in many dales, especially Borrowdale, Buttermere, Langdale, and the Ullswater area. This led to continuing pressures to 'improve' access and to and within most dales, including, for example, road widening and straightening, and the provision of visually intrusive car parks and motor caravan and camping sites. It would take a long time for the national park authority (backed increasingly by public opinion) to begin to turn the tide against this trend.

With regard to improvements to the few major routes, where the emphasis was on through traffic as much as access within the area, even the national park authority was powerless to prevent the major A66 scheme in the northern part of the Lake District going ahead in the late 1960s and early 1970s. Controversies about 'improvements' to the A591 route through the Lakes would also continue post-1945. However, pressure for the creation of a mainly dual-carriageway trunk road, with a bypass of Ambleside, was reduced, but never entirely eliminated, with the opening of the M6, and the completion of the A66 trunk route scheme. A weight limit was then imposed on the Ambleside to Keswick section of the A591, effectively banning heavy goods vehicles from through access. Thus even national park status did not, and does not, guarantee full landscape environmental protection from road 'improvements'.[3]

Electricity and telephones – their landscape impact

It is difficult to imagine life today without the benefits of electricity and the telephone. Both are taken for granted, yet neither existed before the late nineteenth century, and it took many years before all rural areas in

RYDAL.   BEAUTY VALUED
WESTM^D C.C.

WESTM^D C.C.
RYDAL.   A CHARMING FOOTPATH

39 The A591
unimproved. From
FLD archive,
reproduced by kind
permission of Friends
of the Lake District.

A ROAD POLICY
FOR THE
LAKE DISTRICT

Issued by the
FRIENDS OF THE LAKE DISTRICT

40 Widening of A591 south of Thirlspot, north of Thirlmere. Cover from *A Road Policy for the Lake District*, FLD, reprint 1960. From FLD archive, reproduced by kind permission of Friends of the Lake District.

Britain were connected to the electricity and telephone networks: indeed in the Lake District some dales were still without electricity until the 1950s. To generate electricity a power supply is needed (for most of the twentieth century this was predominantly coal), a means of converting it (a power station), and a method of transmitting it through a distribution network. This network – the national, regional and local grids – is predominantly made up of overhead wires carried on metal pylons (for the national and regional high-tension lines) or wooden poles (for local low-tension lines). A local electrical engineer who wrote a regional history of north west electricity boards stated that 'soon stately transmission towers and sweeping power lines added a new feature to the rural landscape'. To which one response was 'No doubt; but although a pylon is a remarkable piece of structural engineering, its intrusion into the countryside is equivalent to the scrawling of a Picasso sketch across a Constable painting'.[4] This latter view was one that FLD took in responding to proposals to introduce electricity and telephone networks in and through the Lake District.

In 1894 the Windermere and District Electrical Supply Company was formed, and by the 1920s was supplying Windermere, Kendal, Grange-over-Sands and Ulverston. At that time the main regional supply sources were the power stations in Barrow-in-Furness and Carlisle. In 1926 the Central Electricity Board was established, charged with building and maintaining a National Grid. FLD did not want to be cast as being against the introduction of electricity, or telephones, into the Lake District, so from the start it responded to proposals on a case-by-case basis with two guiding principles in mind. It wanted routes to be chosen with due regard to their visual impact on the landscape, making them as unobtrusive as possible, and in what were considered the most sensitive areas, it recommended that cables should be laid underground. In many cases power companies and the Central Electricity Board agreed alternative routes, often as a result of site visits by FLD members and

HAWKSHEAD MOOR. RURAL BEAUTY
BY BARROW CORPORATION

BRAITHWAITE. A CAT'S CRADLE
BY MID. CUMB^D ELEC^{TY} SUPPLY CO.

A TRADITIONAL
LAYOUT.
ROSGILL

41 Overhead electric lines 1: better underground? From FLD archive, reproduced by kind permission of Friends of the Lake District.

A MODERN
OVERLAY.
BRAITHWAITE

42 Overhead electric lines 2: contrast. From FLD archive, reproduced by kind permission of Friends of the Lake District.

subsequent meetings with power company and Central Electricity Board staff. For example, in 1935 the Central Electricity Board agreed to reroute a section of the proposed Carlisle–Egremont high-tension line in the Bassenthwaite area to avoid pylons being placed along the east shore of Bassenthwaite into Keswick. They took the pylons to the north of the Skiddaw range and used the existing local grid into Keswick. Success was also achieved in the Ullswater area. The Westmorland and District Electricity Company agreed to place underground about 4½ miles of high-tension line along the eastern and southern Ullswater shoreline between Sandwick Bay, via Place Fell, to Glenridding. Barrow Corporation also agreed to provide underground distribution in Outgate, near Hawkshead, as did the Post Office for telephone connections.

However, one of the most contentious and disputed proposals during this period was the proposed Borrowdale line. It merits closer inspection, because it sums up the dilemma of bringing the benefits of twentieth-century technology into an area of outstanding natural beauty whilst recognising that this involves extra financial cost to minimise its landscape impact. The problem was – and is – who pays the extra costs? The FLD view was that the more profitable parts of an electricity supplier's network should cross-subsidise the extra costs of burying (where appropriate) rural lines.

In September 1937, the Buttermere Slate Quarry entered into a contract with the Mid-Cumberland Electricity Company to receive electric power at its quarry high up on the Honister Pass between Borrowdale and Buttermere. The 11,000 volt power line would run for some 7½ miles on wooden poles 30 to 38 feet in height. Cockermouth Rural District Council (the planning authority) passed the proposed scheme without any objection, although they hoped that the company would meet with objectors over the route. The main objectors were FLD, CPRE and the National Trust. All were in favour of the quarry getting its electricity supply, and they also hoped that Borrowdale households could be included, but they wanted as much as possible of the line to be buried underground.

A first meeting was held on 27 September 1937 between the electricity company and the main objectors to discuss the best – or least bad – route, and the laying of as much of it as possible underground. The power supply company offered two routes for the southern section of the line. Both involved going from Keswick via the eastern side of Catbells, but the first option was thence over National Trust land via the eastern side of Maiden Moor and High Spy, with the alternative taking a route further west behind Castle Crag to Rosthwaite. The company provided costings for overground and underground supply. Initially it also made it clear that it wanted the objectors to pay half the difference between the overground and underground cost.

A FOREGROUND TO CONISTON
BY BARROW CORPORATION

43 Overhead
telephone lines:
better underground?
From FLD archive,
reproduced by kind
permission of Friends
of the Lake District.

A FOREGROUND TO GRASMERE
YARD ARMS BY H.M. POST OFFICE

Naturally enough the objectors wanted professional advice on these costs and also its possible routing up Borrowdale. FLD, acting for itself and on behalf of CPRE, the National Trust and LDSS, engaged W. J. Heywood, a qualified electrical engineer from the Manchester firm of S. H. Heywood, Electrical & Mechanical Engineers. He duly provided his own costings, which were lower than those of the electricity company's, and suggested alternatives. One was to bury the line under the road up Borrowdale. At the next meeting, held on 11 October 1937, discussion took place on routes and costs. The company agreed to re-visit their costings. Meanwhile it had approached Cumberland County Council, which had no part in the planning decision but was asked to comment on the estimates of cost, including the alternative for burying the line under the road.

On 7 November 1937 the County Council expressed the view that the company's extra cost for undergrounding was too high. At another meeting of the company and objectors, on 12 November 1937, it was proposed that the whole route from Hawse End (by Cat Bells) via Grange to Rosthwaite should be put underground with overground lines between Rosthwaite and Seatoller. However, differences in costings remained unresolved. Heywood's figures on behalf of the objectors were now subjected to expert third party review and were confirmed as accurate. On 30 November 1937 the electricity company submitted to Cumberland County Council maps with a revised route and lower costs, and agreed to bear the extra costs of undergrounding itself. The company's figure for this extra undergrounding cost had been £5,061 in September, and was now revised to £2,405: Heywood's figure, throughout, was £717. But the company now only agreed to bury one-third of the high-tension line and none of the low-tension line, and declared its intention of going to apply to the Ministry of Transport for permission to proceed.

The main objectors agreed to write independently to the Ministry of Transport seeking a public inquiry. They were confident in the technical and financial case made by Heywood, their consultant, and wanted to test the general principle of landscape protection in a proposed future national park. The need for such an inquiry was reinforced when the Mid-Cumberland Electricity Company wrote to Cockermouth Rural District Council early in 1938 implying that all its future proposals for electrification schemes would involve overhead transmission lines. However, the company now dropped the scheme, stating that Honister quarry had installed its own private generator. Throughout the dispute both sides had used the media to put over their case. Naturally enough the electricity company (and members of Cockermouth Rural District Council) sought to present the objectors as standing in the way of progress, asserting that they were preventing the benefits of electricity being made available to Borrowdale residents. Heywood, the expert consultant, wrote to Herbert Griffin (secretary of CPRE) on 29 December 1937 that:

> I am, of course, extremely sorry that the scheme is now officially withdrawn by the Supply Company, but I do most strongly feel that the matter should not be allowed to rest there ... I have also been getting what information and advice I can from friends in the supply industry, and from very reliable sources I feel that a representation either to the [Electricity] Commissioners or the Minister, especially if this were backed by a petition from the residents of Borrowdale, requesting a supply irrespective of the Honister Quarries, should be made. I believe if this pressure were properly applied there would be a good chance of the Commission forcing the Mid-Cumberland Electricity Company to take a supply into Borrowdale.

> In view of this I have written Symonds enclosing the draft of a proposed petition (which, of course, he may alter in detail) and I understand that he will get Dr. Bowes, and perhaps some other strong Borrowdale resident, to canvas the whole Valley for support.[5]

It is worth quoting the petition, addressed to the Electricity Commission, Savoy Court, London, in full:

> We, the undersigned residents in Borrowdale, realising with concern the fact that the service of electricity to our houses has apparently been made contingent on the Honister Quarry taking an industrial supply, most strongly petition you to urge the Supply Company to provide a domestic supply for the villages.

> As residents in a valley in which so many depend upon its beauty for a living, it is of great importance to us that no disfigurement of the valley should be allowed. Therefore, whilst pressing for a supply of electricity in our villages, we wish strenuously to urge that the supply be given by means of underground cable. What has been done for Grasmere, a Lake District village famous for the beauty of its situation, can, we hold, be done for the villages of Borrowdale; they have an equal claim.

The petition was circulated and signed by all Borrowdale residents, but only in November 1939 did the parish council receive a reply from the Electricity Commissioners. Unfortunately circumstances had changed by then, and the scheme was held to be uneconomic unless the quarry was included. It would be some time before electric lights could be switched on in Borrowdale homes. In the event this did not happen until 1955–56 when, in spite of the less than wholehearted support of the Lake District Planning Board, the electricity supplier eventually agreed that the whole Borrowdale line should be buried. Meanwhile, during the 1930s the Post

44   Ribbon
development. From
FLD archive,
reproduced by kind
permission of Friends
of the Lake District.

BAD RIBBON DEVELOPMENT
MANOR BROW, KESWICK

TROUTBECK
GOOD COMPOSITION AND LAY-OUT

SEEING BUT SEEN. A COMMON ERROR
CHAPEL STILE.

45 Housing in the landscape: the situation is all. From FLD archive, reproduced by kind permission of Friends of the Lake District.

GARNETT BRIDGE
SNUGLY CONCEALED. THE NATIVE MANNER

AMBLESIDE
A GOOD MODERN HOUSE

46 Ambleside: a good modern house. From FLD archive, reproduced by kind permission of Friends of the Lake District.

Office had arranged, with the agreement of FLD and without any controversy, to bury its telephone lines north of Rosthwaite and around Grange-in-Borrowdale.

Finally, mention should be made of the proposed Kendal to Barrow high-tension transmission line. It was feared that, if and when the full scheme went ahead, the Central Electricity Board would favour a direct route over the southern Lake District via Scout Scar, Bowland Bridge, Gummer's How, Staveley, to Newby Bridge, and thence by the coast to Barrow. Such fears seemed justified when the Central Electricity Board applied to erect high-tension overhead pylons and transmission lines from Kendal to Staveley via Scout Scar. This application was the subject of a public inquiry in 1937. Westmorland County Council and South Westmorland Rural District Council, as well as FLD, objected. The application was refused. When the Central Electricity Board went ahead later, during the Second World War, with the Kendal/Barrow line they routed it as far as possible to the south of the Lake District on low ground around the north side of Morecambe Bay. However, in correspondence between FLD and the Central Electricity Board they said that 'The Friends of the Lake District are influenced by considerations which however desirable in themselves fall largely outside the Board's purview'. The FLD response was 'Nothing could more clearly proclaim the essential conflict between the power of statutory bodies and the needs of an area destined to become a national park'.[6] Controversies over electrification programmes would continue even after the National Park was established in 1951.

There are other stories to tell about FLD during these first formative years. Here in brief are some. In 1936 FLD set up a Lake District Advisory Panel, with the Royal Institute of British Architects. Its purpose was to give free advice on planning and architectural design matters to the public and to local authorities. The emphasis was on trying to secure sympathetic building design in keeping with the Lake District vernacular idiom (see Figures 44–46). FLD also drafted a voluntary code of where, and where not, to build new hostels, club huts, and guest houses (including their recommendations for design). The purpose was to keep daleheads clutter-free in the face of a weak planning framework. In this they largely succeeded. A plan to establish countryside (voluntary) wardens was suggested. This subsequently led to the establishment of Lake District voluntary wardens under the aegis of the Lake District National Park Authority (LDNPA) in 1954, as proposed by Symonds wearing his LDNPA membership hat. In 1938 FLD started a bird watching protection scheme. Finally, also in 1938, the campaign to resolve the problem of pollution of Ullswater by the effluent from Glenridding lead mine started. It dragged on into the 1940s: in 1942 FLD instigated legal action and improvements had taken place by 1944.

Notes

1   See Berry and Beard pp. 22–23.

2

Year	Private Vehicles	Goods Vehicles	Public Transport Vehicles.	All Vehicles
1903	8,000	4,000	5,000	17,000
1909	53,000	30,000	24,000	143,000
1920	187,000	101,000	75,000	591,000
1930	1,056,000	349,000	101,000	2,272,000
1939	2,034,000	488,000	90,000	3,148,000

By comparison out of interest here are some post-1945 figures: -

Year	Private Vehicles	Goods Vehicles	Public Transport Vehicles.	All Vehicles
1950	1,979,000	439,000	123,000	3,970,000
1960	4,900,000	493,000	84,000	8,512,000
1970	9,971,000	545,000	93,000	13,548,000
1980	14,660,000	507,000	110,000	19,199,000
1992	19,870,000	432,000	72,000	24,577,000
2002	24,543,000	425,000	92,000	30,557,000

Source – Department for Transport.

3   The building of the dual-carriageway A590 High and Low Newton bypass, and its opening in 2008, within the southern part of the National Park, provides evidence that full landscape environmental protection remains an aspiration rather than a reality. However, village residents are no doubt happy, as are many of the drivers and passengers that use the A590.

4   W. E. Swale, *Forerunners of the North-Western Electricity Board* (Manchester, 1963) p. 45; in Marshall and Walton, p. 229.

5   CRO (Kendal) WDSO117/B/VI/10/1–5.

6   FLD *Newsletter*, January 1938, pp. 7–8.

47 Steeple with Ennerdale. From FLD archive, reproduced by kind permission of Friends of the Lake District.

CHAPTER SIX

The National Park campaign: 1934–1939

Regions of great natural beauty have a lasting value for the refreshment and inspiration of man. Therefore, the object of creating a national park in the Lake District is to preserve for the future the outward aspect of the district as we see it, with the grand and the beautiful in splendid harmony. The aim is to reserve the Lake District, as we presently have it, for a national 'playground' of body and spirit for the common man: and to hand on as a place of inspiration and refreshment for the poets and artists and philosophers of the future the best mountain sanctuary of the English people.

FLD Pamphlet, *Make the Lake District a National Park*, June 1937.

From its beginnings in 1926 CPRE had been quietly lobbying on behalf of the national park idea. By 1929 it had persuaded the Government formally to consider the issue. Accordingly, the Addison Committee was set up. Each of the Local National Reserve Committees set up under the CPRE umbrella was asked to prepare evidence stating the case for a national park in their particular area. Thus, the Lake District National Reserve Committee (LDNRC) was formed to formulate and give evidence for the Lake District as a prime candidate for national park status. When the Government postponed the consideration of Addison's recommendations, Spence, as secretary of LDNRC, corresponded with Herbert Griffin at CPRE about how the national park flame should be kept alive. As noted in Chapter Two, one tactic, which failed, was to encourage voluntary joint regional planning – as Addison recommended – in the possible Lake District national park area between Lancashire, Cumberland, and Westmorland County Councils. CPRE had rejected the call that all amenity groups who had given evidence to Addison should lobby the Government to press for legislation, but in 1933 Spence enlisted the support of the Bowland-Malhamdale, Cannock Chase, and Dovedale National Reserve Committees to push for a CPRE National Committee on National Parks. At that time, this too was unsuccessful. CPRE felt, with some justice, that the economic and political climate was unfavourable. It was then that Spence, in particular, sought the transformation of the LDNRC into a national public membership amenity group to maintain the campaign for national parks in general and the Lake District in particular. This led to the formation of FLD out of LDNRC in 1934 (see Chapter Two).

After FLD was set up, there was still pressure to provide some form of national park coordinating forum for the various national and local amenity groups throughout the country. CPRE, and especially Herbert Griffin its secretary, was initially reluctant to agree to this. He took the not unreasonable stance that it was already part of CPRE's aims and objectives to push for action on the Addison Report. After all, CPRE had led the pressure for the government to set up the Addison Committee. However, he came round to the view that if such a national forum *was* going to be established, it should logically be under the CPRE umbrella. By 1935 FLD, with Spence and Symonds to the fore, had tried unsuccessfully to resist CPRE control because of then CPRE and FLD differences over the afforestation issue,[1] but this view was soon to change.

At the CPRE annual conference in November 1935 a motion was passed recommending the establishment of a Standing Committee on National Parks (SCNP). Membership was to be confined to national amenity groups alone (such as the National Trust, COSFPS, Cyclists' Tourist Club (CTC) and Youth Hostels Association (YHA)). FLD was regarded in this respect as a local amenity group, albeit one with a national membership. However, it was agreed that the new body could co-opt up to eight other members, and this gave an opportunity for FLD to make its influence felt on the new national body. At the Standing Committee on National Parks meeting of 26 May 1936 it was agreed to co-opt Norman Birkett, Kenneth Spence and E. J. Salisbury. Significantly, Birkett was thence made chairman of SCNP. Other SCNP members who had been, or still were, on FLD's executive committee included Patrick Abercrombie (CPRE), Theo Chorley (National Trust), and Hal Symonds (YHA). Crucially, it was agreed that the committee would be too large and unwieldy as a working group, so a sub-committee, with executive powers, was set up. Kenneth Spence and John Dower were invited to join this new Preparatory Sub-committee. Thus its membership consisted of Norman Birkett (Chairman), Patrick Abercrombie, John Dower, Hal Symonds, Kenneth Spence, Julian Huxley and J. A. Southern. Four out of the SCNP sub-committee of seven also held current posts with FLD. Although direct evidence of how this happened has not been found, the influence of Patrick Abercrombie, representing both CPRE and FLD, could have been important in getting strong FLD representation on SCNP, albeit by indirect means. After all, Abercrombie had always been strongly in favour of national parks and was the driving force behind the establishment of CPRE in 1926. He had had fewer doubts than Herbert Griffin about the creation of FLD, remained a key figure on the CPRE executive committee, and was also technical adviser to FLD as well as an FLD Trustee. Equally importantly, he was well respected professionally and personally by both Kenneth Spence and Herbert Griffin. Furthermore, he acted as an official and unofficial bridge and broker, along with John Dower, between CPRE and FLD when they fell out over tactics during the 1934–1936 afforestation campaign.[2] Of these SCNP sub-committee members, we should single out Hal Symonds and John Dower. Evidence for their key roles in the national park campaign can be found in the records and from the words of their contemporaries at FLD and SCNP.[3]

Norman Birkett (1883–1962) was born in Ulverston and educated at Barrow-in-Furness Grammar School and Emmanuel College, Oxford. He was called to the bar in 1913 and became a famous criminal barrister, being made a Judge of the King's Bench Division in 1941 and serving as one of the panel of judges at the Nuremberg Trials after World War Two. He was appointed to the Privy Council in 1947 and in 1950 was made a Lord Justice of Appeal. He retired in 1957 and was made 1st Baron Birkett in 1958.

48 Norman Birkett KC, MP. Photograph by Elliott & Fry Ltd.

On the creation of FLD, Birkett (along with G. M. Trevelyan) was made a trustee. He then served as president of FLD for 20 years, from 1937 until 1957. As noted above, he was appointed as the first chairman of the CPRE Standing Committee on National Parks, then worked closely with Hal Symonds and John Dower during the national park campaign of the 1930s and 1940s. In spite of his high national and international profile and very time-consuming and active professional career he nevertheless continued throughout his presidency of FLD to take an active interest in Lake District matters. On 8 February 1962, in the House of Lords, he successfully moved to reject a Bill to allow the abstraction of water from Ullswater. He died two days later.

FLD and CPRE, through the cross-representation of key officers such as Symonds, Dower, Birkett and Abercrombie, now worked in concert to lobby the Government to implement the key recommendations of the 1931

Addison Report. They also decided to raise public awareness by publishing suitable pamphlets. Thus by April 1937, Symonds had drafted a proposed FLD Lake District National Park pamphlet, which was agreed by FLD's executive committee: 4,500 copies were printed and distributed in June 1937 under the title *Make the Lake District a National Park: an Appeal to all Lovers of the English Lake District.*[4] Reaction to the pamphlet was not universally favourable. It was inevitable that some local landowners and local authorities expressed their doubts or even their outright opposition to a national park. But, more worryingly, criticism also came from the Herdwick Sheep Breeders Association. Their president spoke against the national parks idea, saying that its advocates were 'people who spent their summers in the district and never saw it the rest of the year', and that a national park 'would mean the whole of the Lake District controlled and run by the state officials' which would 'jeopardise their interests as farmers and landowners'.[5] Canon Wilcox, Chairman of FLD, replied to such criticism, pointing out that FLD's policies were aimed at recognising and preserving traditional dales sheep farming.[6]

At the same time as FLD's pamphlet was being drafted, Dower was preparing a pamphlet on national parks for the SCNP. CPRE published it in mid-1938 under the title *The Case for National Parks in Britain.* The CPRE SCNP also issued a leaflet called *National Parks for Britain – Brief Statement of Policy.* The core contents and recommendations of these publications formed the basis of all future FLD and SCNP proposals until legislation was framed to establish national parks in 1947–1949. There was no wavering on what FLD and CPRE (through SCNP) wanted to see in any future legislation, or why. Tactics employed included the drafting of a National Parks Bill (prepared largely by Symonds and Dower), lobbying the government, and public awareness campaigns. Their success is shown by the fact that John Dower, while working during the Second World War in the Ministry of Town and Country Planning, was asked to write a report on national parks. It was

49 *Make the Lake District a National Park – an appeal to all lovers of the English Lake District,* FLD pamphlet, 1937. From FLD archive, reproduced by kind permission of Friends of the Lake District.

published in 1945,[7] and with other matters relating to the national parks campaign, during and after the Second World War, is considered further in Chapter Eight.

The only difference between FLD and CPRE was one of tone, not substance, although FLD naturally focused on the Lake District, whilst the CPRE canvas was the larger one of England and Wales. The start point was the recognition given in the recommendations of the Addison Committee that the Lake District was a prime candidate for a future national park. Thus for FLD the aim was, as quoted at the beginning of this chapter, to preserve the Lake District as a 'national 'playground of body and spirit for the common man"[8] so that it could be handed on 'as a place of inspiration and refreshment for the poets and artists and philosophers of the future'.[9]

To secure this vision it was argued that a National Parks Commission should be set up 'which will guard and champion natural beauty'. Further 'Like the BBC the Commission will be outside the pressure and influence of politics'. Its powers should be defined by Parliament; it should have a cabinet minister to speak for it in Parliament; and have the power to override decisions of other government departments and bodies where conflict occurred between national park aims and their development proposals. The National Parks Commission (NPC) should also receive and deploy public funds without change to the current local government system. The pamphlet ends with a paragraph entitled 'London and the Lake District' which makes interesting reading:

> We HAVE national parks, though we forget it. Every year a quarter of a million pounds is spent on the maintenance of Hyde Park, St. James' and the Green Park, Kew Gardens and a half dozen other of the chief delights of London. And these are paid for by the tax payer – the scheme we have been advocating – not by London rates. True, these London parks are tamed, not wild: their beauty is more of art than nature. But they are a precedent of some force. For those who live hard lives in Whitehaven and Maryport and Cleator Moor, being taxpayers, are therefore shareholders in Hyde Park for the benefit of Londoners. Could not the nation, by a similar fund for the "maintenance" – not expropriation – of the Lake District, become a shareholder at long last in that, for the benefit of ALL? (see Figure 50).

The thorny issue of the relationship between the proposed NPC and local government was somewhat fudged at this stage. The important thing was to get national government to agree that legislation should be brought forward as soon as possible, so that National Parks Commissions for England and Wales should be established. The 1937 FLD pamphlet made clear that their proposals did not involve any change in local government structures, but that the NPC should have the duty to protect the Lake

YOU PAY TAXES FOR THIS.
KENSINGTON GARDENS. A NATIONAL PARK

THE LAKE DISTRICT. NOT A NATIONAL PARK.
NO TAXES PROTECT ITS BEAUTY

50 Funding the parks: Kensington Gardens and Lake District. Symonds on rocks (lower picture). From FLD archive, reproduced by kind permission of Friends of the Lake District.

District National Park by having a stronger development planning function. It was claimed that the current town and country planning law was too weak and, in any case, not working well at local government level. In particular, the attempt at joint planning between Lancashire, Westmorland and Cumberland County Councils had failed. There was the sticky issue of whether joint planning could be made to work at all, or whether there should be a unitary planning authority for the future national park area. Thinking on this was to develop in the 1940s. Finally, the issue of financial compensation was addressed: potential loss of land value as a result of stricter control over development was to be met by a new compensation fund controlled by the NPC, to be financed from national taxation not local rates.

These core proposals were to emerge largely intact, with much more added in the way of detail, in the recommendations of the two government-appointed committees into national parks at the end of the Second World War (Dower in 1945 and Hobhouse in 1947). However, the outcome of these, in the form of the National Parks and Access to the Countryside Act of 1949, was, in the view of FLD (and Symonds especially) and CPRE, a disappointment and was regarded as a lost opportunity that resulted in less effective national parks. That is jumping ahead. Meanwhile, credit is due to FLD and CPRE (through the SCNP) for not only keeping the national park torch alight throughout the 1930s, but also influencing proposals on where the first national parks should be located in England and Wales, and why, and how, they should be organised.

FLD should also take credit for playing a major role in suggesting the national park boundaries. Symonds confirms this: 'Our original boundaries were the work of our first Honorary Planning Advisor, Sir Patrick Abercrombie, of his successor in that office, John Dower, and of Kenneth Spence and the present chairman [Symonds] of the society.'[10] There have always been different views on where the 'Lake District' starts and finishes.[11] The consensus is that it certainly encompasses the central core of higher fell country and their associated dales radiating from it, many with a lake or lakes. It can be likened to a cartwheel with its hub and spokes. To continue the analogy, the problem is not so much deciding how many spokes the wheel has, but rather in deciding the size of the wheel. In other words, where does the Lake District 'stop'? This issue became more than a debating point when decisions were required regarding the actual area of land to be included in a future national park. This was obviously a matter of opinion, not fact, but suitable criteria, although subjective, were required to inform this process.[12]

Potential candidates for national parks, including their likely boundaries, were first put forward by CPRE, on behalf of all local national reserve committees, to the Addison Committee in 1929 (see Chapter Two). The map of the potential Lake District park area and its boundaries was largely the work of Abercrombie.[13] A map of the future national park area, including its broad boundaries, was then included in the 1934 public pamphlet to launch FLD (see Chapter Two). This map would henceforth appear on the front cover of the annual FLD *Report*

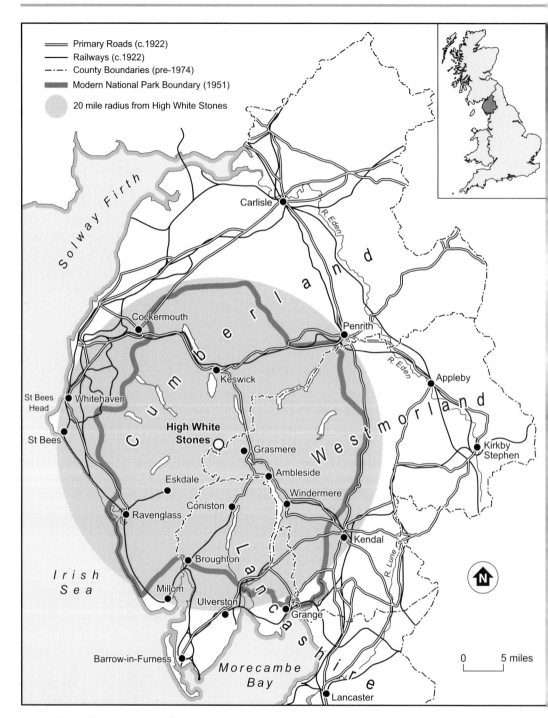

MAP 4 High White Stones and 1951 National Park boundaries. From FLD archive, reproduced by kind permission of Friends of the Lake District. Map redrawn by Simon Chew, Lancaster Environment Centre.

and Newsletter, and on that of the 1937 FLD national park pamphlet. By the early 1930s, it was agreed that the central point of the national park would be based on High White Stones,[14] about 1½ miles north of the Langdale Pikes. Spence and Symonds variously described an area with a radius of 15 to 20 miles from High White Stones as outer limits for national park boundaries. Spence thought that a ten mile radius from High White Stones 'would take in all that the casual visitor thinks of as the Lake District' (see Map 4). Nevertheless, he recommended a 20 mile radius because 'we must remember the importance of maintaining an equally stringent supervision of the fringe area which is, by its very physical nature, much more liable to be 'developed' – and so spoilt by short-sighted exploitation'.[15] Symonds makes reference to a 15 mile radius in his book on afforestation.[16] In the event, this 15 mile radius was adopted by FLD and included in its national park pamphlet[17] and, outlined by Spence,[18] would subsequently be the basis of further more detailed discussion and fine-tuning by Symonds and Dower during the 1940s (see Chapter Eight).

Conclusion

What shape was FLD in by the start of the Second World War? As a new amenity body it was thriving. Nearly 600 members signed up on FLD formation in 1934. Annual individual subscribers rose from 1,300 in 1935 to 1,950 in 1936, 2,400 in 1937 and 2,600 in 1938. It was thought by Symonds at the time that membership would probably plateau at 2,500 (by comparison CPRE membership numbers were 1,082 in 1936, 1,201 in 1937, and 1,245 in 1938). Local FLD branches were established in Whitehaven, Keswick, Penrith, Windermere, Manchester, Leeds, Birmingham, Liverpool, London, Cambridge, and Oxford. However, only the Leeds branch survived the Second World War.[19] Finances were sound. Annual subscriptions were set at 2s 6d: life membership was £5.

The first full-time employee, an assistant treasurer/secretary, was Miss A. J. Newbiggin: she started in 1937 and was paid £220 per annum. A typewriter and duplicator were purchased for her use and from then on minutes were typed not handwritten. During 1937 a lease was taken out on office premises at 2, Midland Chambers, Ambleside. Executive committee members were unpaid volunteers – as they remain to this day. They all contributed their time, knowledge and expertise as they could.

As well as those people already mentioned, attention should be drawn to the work that Roland Wade carried out during this period. For a while he continued a footpaths survey virtually single-handed and then began a survey of commons using OS 6-inch maps. He spent many weekends and other spare time travelling from Leeds to the Lake District. These

maps, although uncompleted, were nevertheless an immense help to FLD
in their dealings with the new National Park Authority when it was given
the duty to prepare rights of way maps for the national park area in the
early 1950s. Roland Wade subsequently became FLD chairman from 1970
to 1980.

It might reasonably have been thought that with the coming of war in
September 1939 the spotlight might have been literally turned off FLD
and its key objective to win support for the creation of a Lake District
National Park. However, as we shall see, whilst the war was being fought,
minds at national level became focused on the sort of 'home' to which
heroes should return after it was successfully concluded. Politicians of all
parties would now become more sympathetic to the idea of preserving
and giving access to the best parts of its landscape for all to enjoy. This
was in fact the opportunity that the supporters of national parks were
looking for. In this regard CPRE (with FLD) was in a very strong
position to have a major influence. They used this opportunity to good
effect.

Notes

1   FLD Executive Committee Minutes 10 January 1936.

2   FLD was finally given formal recognition as a constituent society of the SCNP at the
      end of 1945. Lady Chorley was the first official FLD representative – See FLD
      Minutes 8 December 1945.

3   See especially FLD Minutes and Dower/Symonds correspondence in FLD Archives
      CRO (Kendal) WDSO/117/Box 68 and 107.

4   *Make the Lake District a National Park. An appeal to all lovers of the English Lake
      District* (FLD, 1937).

5   *Westmorland Gazette* 25 February 1939.

6   *Westmorland Gazette* 4 March 1939.

7   'Report on National Parks in England and Wales' (HMSO, Cmnd 6378).

8   FLD National Park Pamphlet (FLD, 1937), p. 2.

9   Ibid, p.2.

10   FLD *Report and Newsletter*, September 1951, p. 9.

11   For an excellent account of the history of Lake District 'boundaries' see S. M. Clark,
      'Perceptions of the boundaries of the Lake District from 18th century, to the
      designation of the National Park', Unpublished Diploma Dissertation, University of
      Lancaster, 1994.

12   Of course, the same question arose, or arises, in any part of the country which was,
      or is, being considered for national park status, or indeed any other 'special'
      designation.

13   See Clark, pp. 30–32.

14   Ordnance Survey maps, including editions of the 1920s and 1930s, have always
      named the actual highest point here as High Raise (762 metres, app. 2,500 feet) with
      High White Stones named just alongside.

[15]   C. Williams-Ellis (ed.), *Britain and the Beast* (London: J. M. Dent & Sons Ltd., 1937), Chapter Nine; K. Spence, *The Lakes*, pp. 244–245.

[16]   'To speak roughly, the *central* Lake District lies inside a circle drawn with a radius of 15 miles from a centre at High White Stones (just north of the Langdale Pikes). This gives a total area of just over 700 square miles'; H. H. Symonds, *Afforestation in the Lake District* (London: J. M. Dent & Sons Ltd., 1936), footnote 2, p. 22.

[17]   'The essential Lake District, its central and mountainous area, lies all within a circle drawn from a point one mile north of Langdale Pikes as centre and with a radius of 15 miles'. *Make the Lake District a National Park, An Appeal to all lovers of the English Lake District* (FLD, 1937).

[18]   'This leaves the coast at Seascale, follows round the foot of the fells near Egremont, and along the main Egremont-Cockermouth road. It excludes Cockermouth urban district and makes up behind Binsey to take in Uldale and Ireby and Caldbeck; from there it runs south-east to take in Greystoke and Dacre but excludes the urban district of Penrith. It then roughly follows the A6 south over Shap to Kendal, which town is also excluded; it continues south to Levens before turning east to the Kent estuary and Morecambe Bay. It includes Grange and the whole Cartmel peninsula, but crosses the Furness peninsula just north of Ulverston to exclude the mining and manufacturing area surrounding Barrow, Dalton, Ulverston, and Askam. Crossing Duddon Sands it excludes the small isolated mining town of Millom, and regains the coast of the Irish Sea west of Haverigg Point'. (ed.) Clough-Ellis, Spence, Chapter Nine, p. 245.

[19]   'Watchers' were also set up in various parts of the Lake District to be the "eyes and ears" of FLD on the ground reporting any 'undesirable development' proposals.

51 Blea Tarn and Langdale Pikes. From FLD archive, reproduced by kind permission of Friends of the Lake District.

CHAPTER SEVEN

The Second World War years and after: 1940–1951

> *We have not been able, as we desired, to arrange members' concerted help in critical causes, for under the Defence Regulations it is impossible to organise public opposition to official schemes – for this would reveal the nature of them and their whereabouts. In effect, propaganda and press correspondence are dead … our silence has covered action, not inaction … we are necessarily not in the papers: but we are not out of action, and have no intention of becoming so.*
>
> Rev H. H. Symonds, *FLD Report and Annual Report*, 1940.

The way in which FLD carried out its business during the Second World War between 1939 and 1945 and in the immediate post-war years is now examined, together with the methods used to lobby against and influence the outcome of proposals for change it saw as undesirable.

As far as individual membership was concerned, numbers fell from 2,600 in 1938 to 2,200 in 1939. Following a further fall, to 1,900 in 1940, the figure stabilised at around 1,600 for the duration of hostilities. From an organisational viewpoint, executive committee membership was surprisingly stable: bluntly, most were beyond the front-line military service age range, which afforded a measure of continuity. Lord Howard of Penrith died in 1939 and was succeeded as president by Norman Birkett. At the first meeting to be held after the declaration of war, on 22 September 1939, 'It was decided that in order to have daylight these should be held during the winter at mid-day, with lunch at the White Lion Hotel (Windermere); and that the dates and frequency of such meetings be left to the judgement of the officers'. The blackout had arrived. In fact the established pre-war cycle of executive committee meetings was to continue from 1942. The venues were alternately the Rigg's Hotel, Windermere and the Sun Hotel, Ulverston. In his first message to members in his new role as FLD president, Norman Birkett wrote in the 1940 *Newsletter and Annual Report*:

> I should like to send a special word to members at this most difficult time. The supreme issues which are being decided in this war demand

from everybody all that can be given in time and work and devotion. Nothing must come before that great and overmastering duty, and considerations of the national safety and well-being must override everything else. Our activities are necessarily and inevitably restricted.

To budget for a reduced income, the Ambleside office was sub-let to the end of the tenancy, only storage room was taken there, and the clerical staff were released. FLD was extremely fortunate to have Hal Symonds as secretary. He moved from Grasmere to Eskdale in 1939 and thereafter undertook all FLD administrative duties virtually unaided and unpaid on a full-time basis as well as carrying out his other local and national campaigning roles and duties. He was, and would remain for many years, the driving force of FLD.

In spite of the temporary removal of overt and public campaign tactics, during the war years FLD influence, through its key people and their networks at local and national levels, really paid off. Symonds put it neatly: 'It is of no use in these days to attempt public propaganda or meetings, and the only effective propaganda which can be done now for our ideal of a national park is in the circles of government'.[1] At this point something more should be said about John Dower, because his role

52 John Dower (undated). Private Collection.

during and after the war was pivotal. Working as a temporary civil servant he was the key link between FLD at local level (with Symonds as secretary), CPRE at national level (through the SCNP, with Birkett – FLD president – as chairman and Symonds as hon. drafting secretary) and relevant ministers, MPs, and other civil servants in central government.

John Dower (1900–1947)[2] was born in 1900 at Ilkley, Yorkshire. He was educated at Leys School, Cambridge, and Cambridge University (St. John's College) where he read history and then architecture, establishing his own architectural practice in 1931. He was particularly interested in the new field of aerodrome design and was a keen supporter of various outdoor movements. At one stage he was president of the Ramblers' Association, and he designed the youth hostels at Malham (Yorkshire), Eskdale (Cumbria) and Bellingham

(Northumberland). We have already seen that he was a friend of Kenneth Spence, and that he wrote and read Spence's obituary at his memorial service in Manchester Cathedral in 1944; that he was responsible for getting FLD launch material published and printed in 1934; and for drawing up the 'red line' map, the basis for the forestry exclusion zone agreed between CPRE and the Forestry Commission in 1936. He was also the first hon. drafting secretary to the CPRE SCNP, drafting their pamphlet *The Case for National Parks* published in 1938.

At the outset of the Second World War Dower was an FLD committee member and FLD hon. technical advisor – following on from Patrick Abercrombie. He was now 39 years of age and a member of the Officer Reserve (Royal Engineers). He joined the army as war broke out, but contracted tuberculosis and was invalided out. In August 1942 he was appointed to a small unit in the Ministry of Works and Planning responsible for the planning of post-war reconstruction. During this period Dower was able to use his role as a temporary civil servant to inform and influence future government policy on the creation of national parks, and to act as a link between Symonds and relevant ministers and government departments on specific FLD matters of local concern. This is demonstrated in the account of the Calgarth seaplane factory campaign below. Dower was given responsibility for overseeing rural policy and, specifically, for carrying out an enquiry into national park areas. The Scott Report on *Land Utilisation in Rural Areas* (1942) gave strong endorsement to the national park principle. In the light of this, Dower was asked to prepare a longer report on national parks for circulation among government departments. This was done in 1943. By 1944 he was working in the Ministry of Town and Country Planning, and in May 1945, following consent from the Cabinet's Reconstruction Committee, W. S. Morrison, Coalition Government Minister of Town and Country Planning, asked Dower to convert his internal report into a White Paper for general publication and public comment. The Dower Report, *National Parks in England and Wales*, London, HMSO, Cmd 6628 (1945) was the template for the subsequent Hobhouse Report. Dower served on this committee.

Tragically, Dower died, aged 47, in October 1947, a mere three months after the Hobhouse report was published as a White Paper. In a very real sense his legacy can be judged by the fact that Hobhouse's Report was said to be 'Dower Report Two'. As a memorial to him the former Countryside Agency headquarters in Cheltenham, now a Natural England regional office, is named John Dower House.

How did FLD go about lobbying against what they saw as undesirable developments, particularly during the war period when they were often instigated under wartime emergency Defence Regulations? In order to answer this question, two examples of changes in land use will be examined in more detail: the Calgarth Park seaplane factory and housing scheme and the military use of the Lake District.

Calgarth Seaplane Factory and housing scheme

The case of the Calgarth Park seaplane factory demonstrates very well how FLD used behind-the-scenes campaigning techniques during the war, and more public ones after it. It also raises the issue of what is appropriate development in a national park once a precedent is set. The story can be summarised as follows. In May 1940 the 'phoney war' ended when Germany invaded France and Belgium, followed by the evacuation of the British armed forces from Dunkirk, and the Battle of Britain. When Churchill became prime minister, Beaverbrook was given responsibility for aircraft production, and it was agreed to disperse this to secure its safety from bombing raids. Two suitable sites for a seaplane factory and hanger and accompanying housing accommodation were identified at White Cross Bay, Calgarth, on the eastern shores of Windermere, near Troutbeck Bridge (see Map 5). It had previously been agricultural land and was not zoned for industrial development. Over 200 houses were also to be built on a 45-acre site for factory workers. Neither FLD nor CPRE could object to the proposals in public or in private, but instead they used contacts within Westminster and Whitehall to lobby the government and make the case for the removal of the factory and housing as soon as possible after the war.

In this they were successful. The key was a written promise extracted from the government at the time that the scheme was proposed, in 1940.[3] Without this things might have turned out very differently, and the role of Symonds at FLD and Herbert Griffin at CPRE, and their united stand in dealing with government, was pivotal. This was despite the fact that when communications between FLD and CPRE and FLD/CPRE and government began in November 1940 the London Blitz was underway and Griffin had to remove CPRE operations (including all files and records) out of London to the West Country. It was also crucial that Norman Birkett and Patrick Abercrombie were at that time official advisers to the government on various matters and that John Dower became a temporary civil servant working inside Whitehall. Therefore, it is worth examining the events of this period in a little more detail, giving a fascinating insight into 'how things got done' behind the scenes at a time when secrecy was essential to protect the war effort.

FLD's executive committee first considered the Calgarth proposal at its meeting of 27 November 1940. Symonds reported that he had 'invited the assistance of certain members and friends of the society in interviewing the relevant Service Departments in London, and that Mr. Nunn and others had in hand the matter of a Parliamentary Question'.

MAP 5 Map of
Windermere,
reproduced from 1958
Ordnance Survey
map.

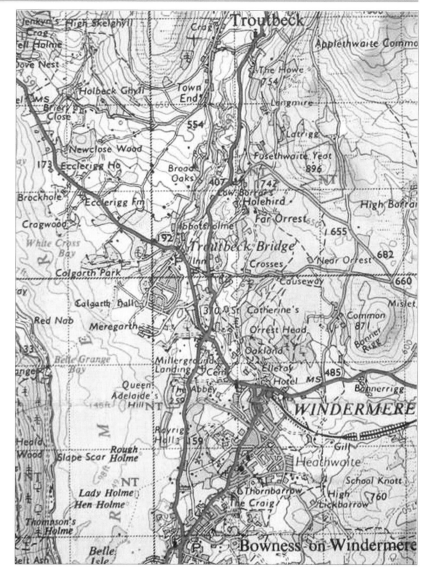

He was already in contact with key members of FLD's National Council, a body set up at the birth of FLD in 1934 to act as a group of influential supporters who could be relied upon to lobby and support as appropriate. Members included George Strauss, M.P., and John Dower, at that time working as a civil servant in the Ministry of Works and Buildings. Symonds also communicated regularly with Herbert Griffin, still CPRE secretary. It was agreed that pressure should be put on the government to find an alternative site, but if this failed Symonds was to send a letter to the relevant government departments to obtain an assurance that all buildings should be removed as soon as possible after the war was ended. Griffin at CPRE did likewise. CPRE and FLD

worked together harmoniously. After much to-ing and fro-ing in the government and between it and FLD/CPRE, a seemingly positive result emerged. A letter dated 20 January 1941 was sent to Symonds at FLD and Griffin at CPRE from the Ministry of Aircraft Production,[4] signed by a senior civil servant, Col. J. J Llewellin. It was marked 'Secret', and in it, Llewellin stated that he had met George Strauss, M.P., and had told him that:

> a question in the House [of Commons] could not in the present circumstances be effective ... because the last thing that we (and I assume the people of Windermere) want is to tell the enemy where this factory is going to be situated.

He says that he is writing on behalf of Lord Beaverbrook, the Minister of Aircraft Production, and that:

> I am, therefore, glad to repeat that I have Lord Beaverbrook's authority to say that we undertake to have these buildings taken down as soon as the military situation makes it safe to do so at the end of the war. A slipway will be constructed and my undertaking does not extend to taking that up ....

53 The first Short Sunderland (DP176) built at Windermere ready for launching in front of the main hanger on 10th September 1942. The workforce has been assembled outside to watch the launch. The aircraft is on its beaching gear and the nose turret is winched back in the mooring position. Reproduced courtesy of Peter Greetham, via Allan King.

We have no wish to make Windermere a permanent industrial centre. The houses, you will be glad to hear, have been deleted from the scheme. We hope to house any men whom we bring from the South in hostels, hotels or by billeting them.

The decision on housing was to change quickly, and it became an integral part of the scheme. At this stage Symonds and Dower were in discussions about tactics. Dower wrote to Symonds on 24 May 1941,[5] sending him two letters – one typed and one handwritten. The former was an 'official' letter from his workplace in the Ministry of Works and Buildings, the latter from his home address in Hampstead, London. Copies of both letters were also sent to Griffin at CPRE. In the formal letter, Dower outlined details of the proposed housing accommodation that his department would undertake on behalf of the Aircraft Production Ministry, and stated that the Ministry knew nothing of the 'Beaverbrook offer' to remove all buildings after the war finished. He rectified this by quoting the relevant parts of the offer in his current letter and sending a copy of it to the senior civil servant in his department, as well as to CPRE and George Strauss, M.P. Perhaps of more interest is what Dower wrote in the handwritten personal letter:

> this a strictly confidential postscript to my not quite so confidential letter. The question is what do you, Griffin and Strauss do about it?

He then went on to say:

> I don't think there's any chance of you stopping the scheme: it seems pretty clear that it is regarded as urgently war-necessary … you might press for some other site: but I don't think you would succeed … I suggest, therefore, that the line to take, with the utmost firmness, is that the housing scheme as a whole, like the factory, is covered by the promise "to have the buildings taken down as soon as the military situation makes it safe." This line should be taken with M.A.P. [Ministry of Aircraft Production], in the first instance, not with the M.W.B. [Ministry of Works and Buildings] who are merely the agents of the M.A.P. (and had not been informed by them of any promises).

Much more haggling over the precise nature of the undertaking took place during 1941 and early 1942. Eventually the original pledge was amended by the Ministry of Aircraft Production in March 1942 to read:

> I think I cannot do better than to reiterate the promise that Colonel Llewellin, my predecessor in this office, gave in relation to the factory, that we will have whatever accommodation is erected to house the work people at the factory removed as soon as the Ministry of Health is satisfied that the housing needs of other parts of the country no longer make advisable the retention of this temporary housing

accommodation in the Lake District. In implementing this undertaking as to the housing estate consultation will be held with the Friends of the Lake District and the Council for the Preservation of Rural England.

54 Overhead view of Calgarth Estate. Reproduced courtesy of Laura Pogson.

Symonds and Griffin had worked hard behind the scenes to secure this promise.

After the war, FLD and CPRE made sure that the agreement was honoured in spite of a change in government. However, there was local support for retention of both the factory and the housing accommodation on a more permanent basis. A petition was raised by the Calgarth Residents' Association. In 1947 Windermere Urban District Council purchased the land and they, too, wanted to retain the housing. FLD and CPRE successfully challenged local opposition, this time with the full support of the government, including the new prime minister, Clement Attlee.

It took until 1949 for the factory, hanger, and other outbuildings to be demolished; but the extensive concrete foundations remained *in situ*. The housing issue dragged on into the 1960s, until compromises were reached. Demolition of houses began as late as 1954 when residents were found alternative local authority accommodation in the Windermere area. Much of the land area occupied by 'temporary' housing was gradually restored to agricultural use, but by then the north-east part of the site had been earmarked for a new secondary school and other parts for new housing. The factory's concrete foundations remained because the cost of removing them was deemed too high. In this state, the land could not revert to agricultural use, so the owner obtained permission to develop the land as a caravan site, originally just for touring caravans, but later for fixed ones as well. FLD at the time thought it the best of a bad job as it was directly off the main A591 road and not in a remote area. This site has subsequently become a major static caravan park, albeit as well landscaped and out of sight of Windermere as can be achieved.[6]

The Lake District and the war effort

During the Second World War the Lake District was home to military training areas and associated camps, ordnance factories, airfields and gunnery ranges. FLD could hardly be seen to object to these developments. Plainly the armed forces needed to be trained properly; they also needed suitable arms and ammunition. However, early pressure was put on the War Department to ensure that the sites were deemed to be only temporary and the case was made for their removal after the war. The problem was that the government could – and in some cases did – invoke the use of the Defence Acts of 1842 and 1854, which allowed for the compulsory purchase in secret of land for military purposes. However, FLD and CPRE persuaded the government to use its own Defence Regulations 51 and 52, granting temporary possession of land for military purposes during emergencies. The problem was to ensure that 'temporary' did not become 'permanent'.

Several major developments took place during the war. Two areas were identified for military training: Martindale (3,000 acres, with a camp at Glenridding), and Kirby, Blawith and Ulpha Fells (12,000 acres). Royal Ordnance Factories were built on the western side of the Lake District at Sellafield, Drigg and Bootle, and a small, and well-landscaped, water pumping station was constructed at the south-west end of Wastwater to provide a water supply for the Drigg Royal Ordnance Factory. A gunnery range was established at Eskmeals on the western coast; a bombing target range was located in the Duddon estuary; RAF airfields and camps were established at Cark, Millom and Haverigg; and finally in 1944 an RAF transmitter tower and electricity line were erected on Black Combe.

In 1947, the Labour Government published a *Services' Land Requirements* White Paper to cover the whole country. In commenting on its proposals, FLD noted that a high proportion of proposed areas were in the higher hill country of northern England. Furthermore, there was a presumption that existing areas used during wartime might continue on a more permanent basis. Against this background FLD had to adopt its stance: there would have to be give and take.

In December 1944, FLD adopted a policy of seeking the restoration to non-industrial use of the coastline from Sellafield to the Esk estuary. This was because that area was proposed, as first mentioned in the *Cumbrian Regional Report* of 1932 and subsequently endorsed by FLD, for inclusion in a future Lake District National Park. However, after the war was over in 1945, Sellafield Royal Ordnance Factory was offered to Courtaulds, a textile company. By 1947 Courtaulds did not want to take up this offer, and the site was subsequently converted to an 'atomic research station' (initially called Windscale). FLD raised concerns but no major objections to this development, and Patrick Abercrombie was asked by FLD to approach the Royal Fine Arts Commission for its views on the materials, colour and shape of the proposed 400-foot high chimney (furthermore, FLD merely 'noted' the application for a second 400-foot chimney in 1949). The point was that FLD had by then conceded that any future national park boundary should lie further south, in exchange for a firm promise to close down and remove the Drigg and Bootle Royal Ordnance Factories and restore their sites. The most that FLD achieved during this period was to avoid the Drigg site being used as an extension of Windscale (and thus for atomic research) and to secure the demolition and removal of Bootle Royal Ordnance Factory and the restoration of its site. FLD had less success in preventing the extension of the Eskmeals gun range but, as a result of a public inquiry, it managed to secure concessions to limit the range to seawards firing with time and date restrictions. In 1948 the RAF agreed to abandon the Millom range and airfield, and the transmitter and electricity line on Black Combe were subsequently removed.

Persuading the Army to agree to abandon its use of Martindale and the Kirby, Blawith and Ulpha fells military training areas was more difficult, and patience and tenacity were required. By 1946, in advance of *Services, Land Requirements* White Paper, the War Department was considering the permanent use of both areas. FLD and CPRE undertook an active press campaign, as well as lobbying parliament and the ministry. At the same time, the Department identified Langdale and Bowderdale in the northern Howgills (to the east of the Lake District) as a potential new field firing area, as well as nearly 4,000 acres of Crosby Ravensworth Fell north of the Howgills as a potential armoured training area. FLD had a site meeting with military staff in Langdale and, together with CPRE SCNP, 'reluctantly' came to the conclusion that these areas should be 'traded' for Martindale. Indeed, this was the stance that FLD took at the subsequent public inquiry into the two proposals, unlike Westmorland County Council which opposed both. In the event, the proposals were withdrawn in 1948, the army relinquished Martindale, and the Glenridding camp was demolished in 1949. After further campaigning and negotiation the Ulverston training area was also abandoned. Both sites reverted to their previous land use. Once the new army regional command structure was in place, the forces settled for a major concentration and extension of the Warcop training area in the Eden Valley and adjacent Pennines, where the army remains to this day.

This is not quite the end of the story. In the south of the Lakes, parts of the Cartmel peninsula, originally proposed by Dower and Hobhouse for inclusion in the future national park, had been occupied for military purposes during the war; in particular, Cark airfield. After 1949 various proposals were put forward to extend activities. These included the permanent military use of Cark airfield, an anti-tank firing range at Rougholme Point/Humphrey Head, and an anti-aircraft training battery at Cowpren Point. Eventually all proposals were abandoned with the exception of the proposed Rougholme Range. However, after more campaigning, the War Ministry agreed to the re-alignment of the range and allowed open public access to Humphrey Head, with the whole site to be abandoned and cleared by 1952. The Duddon estuary bombing range was abandoned in 1948.

Symonds summed the situation up thus:

> One may feel that in striving to rescue the Lake District from Defence Regulations 51 & 52 something quite definite, if not all, has been achieved. The conflict is exacting. Mary Tudor forecast that, when she died, CALAIS would be found engraved on her heart: those engaged in the campaign just recorded – or rather in a very brief outline hinted – may, in an elegy written in a like place, one day disclose the runic lettering D.R. 51/52.[7]

However, although the military use of land may have waxed and waned during the 1940s, other potential major landscape changes were emerging after the war ended. Therefore, before we move on to consider the role of FLD as a major 'spear-carrier' for the national park movement during the 1940s, we should briefly outline some of these proposals, focused on the vexed issues of water abstraction and the potential for hydro-electricity power generation in the Lake District.

New reservoirs had been created out of the natural lakes at Thirlmere and Haweswater for the water needs of Manchester during the 1890s and 1930s respectively. The Haweswater scheme was approved by Act of Parliament in 1919, before the formation of FLD. Thus FLD could only comment on its design details and landscaping when construction of the dam and the flooding of Mardale began in the late 1930s. Before 1945 water abstraction for the needs of the west coast towns had largely been met without major visual changes to the Lake District, using Coniston, Wastwater, Crummock Water, Loweswater, and Ennerdale Water. Embankments and water draw-down were on a minor scale and visually unobtrusive. This approach was to change after 1945. Lancashire County Council and Cumberland County Council carried out a review of future water demand and supply, and a firm proposal was made to raise the level of Ennerdale Water by some five feet, in readiness for the takeover by Courtaulds of the Royal Ordnance Factory at Sellafield. It went to a public inquiry and was given the 'green light'. But, as noted above, Courtaulds never relocated and the scheme was dropped. Ennerdale Water survived unscathed at this time, but renewed proposals for water abstraction schemes would occur in the future. Moreover, possible new reservoirs were to be considered for Loweswater and nearby Mosedale, as well as Caldew Head (north of Skiddaw). FLD objected to the first two but agreed to give qualified support to the Caldew Head proposal. In the event none of them came to fruition. Meanwhile, the Duddon valley was under what FLD considered a double threat to its natural beauty. First, a possible new reservoir north of Seathwaite Church with a 30-foot high dam was proposed, and second, a major hydro-electric power scheme was the subject of a technical study. At that time there was a major expansion of hydro-electric power schemes in the mountain areas of Scotland and in Snowdonia, and many subsequently went ahead.

The technical report relating to the Eskdale and the Duddon Valley hydro-electric power scheme stated that:

> The most prolific area of the Lake District is located about the River Duddon and the headwaters of the Esk where, locally, the average rainfall reaches 180 inches or more. Suitable reservoir sites are found at different levels on the Esk and the Duddon, to which further water can be collected by tunnelling, so that a stage-by-stage scheme is possible, and has been prepared and put forward for consideration, using an aggregate head of 1,260 feet with the lowest station discharging nearly at sea-level. Three power-stations along the main course of the waterflow, and a separate power-station to develop a lateral fall from a small area with its own reservoir storage would provide a total installation of 48,600 kilowatts with an annual output of more than 120 million kilo-watt hours.[8]

All this would have involved substantial new infrastructure. First, there would be two reservoirs on the Upper Esk, one located under the Cam Spout shoulder of Scafell, and the other located above the Esk Falls in Lingcove Beck under Bowfell. Two access roads would be constructed. From these reservoirs the water would be tunnelled to the upper Duddon valley, in which there would be three sets of reservoirs, and three power stations all linked by an overground steel water pipe and transmission lines for the electricity produced, with transformer stations and switchgear buildings en route. In addition to these new man-made features, the flow of the Esk and the Duddon would be much reduced for most of the year. Whatever one's current views on the need for more renewable energy, if this scheme had gone ahead the Upper Esk and the whole of the Duddon valley landscape would have been altered dramatically. The rationale was to supplement or replace Barrow's existing coal-fired power station. However, the economics and politics were in favour of cheaper coal-generated electricity rather than more expensive water-generated electricity, so the scheme stayed permanently in a file. FLD's view was that after the threat from afforestation had been seen off, the upper Esk and Duddon valleys had again been saved from inappropriate major landscape change.

The development proposals considered in this chapter – and others – confirmed FLD's view of how weak and fragmented the existing planning framework was, reinforcing its argument that a Lake District National Park with a strong planning framework was urgently needed.

Notes

1   FLD *Annual Report and Newsletter.* 1941, p. 2.

2   Professor Michael Dower, one of John Dower's sons, provided information to the author about his father's life in exchanges of communication in January 2006. He sent copies of two articles and two pictures of his father. One was an obituary by L. J. Watson written for the publication by Tom Stephenson *Out of Doors* in the Winter 1947 edition; the other was a draft text by John Sheail prepared for the *Dictionary of National Biography*, annotated with notes and suggested amendments by Robin Dower, John's other son and Michael's brother.

3   Section 51(3) of the 1945 Requisitioned Land Act, which included the restoration of the Calgarth sites, then subsequently reinforced this.

4   CRO (Kendal) WDSO 117/B/VI/32.

5   CRO (Kendal) WDSO 117/B/VI/32.

6   The CPRE Archives, lodged at the Museum of English Rural Life, University of Reading, contain four very thick files on the Calgarth saga (SR CPRE C/1/36/4–7). The Calgarth story is also told at length in the FLD Archives lodged at CRO (Kendal) (WDSO 117/B/VI/32). For a fascinating social history of the Calgarth factory and housing estate, with photos and interviews with many of the inhabitants who lived there during and after the war, see: Allan King, *Wings on Windermere: the history of the Lake District's forgotten flying boat factory* (Poland, Stratus, 2009); www.flyingboats.org

7   FLD *Annual Report and Newsletter.* 1948, p. 9.

8   See FLD *Annual Report and Newsletter.* 1950, pp. 4–5.

55 Scafell range from Gable. From FLD archive, reproduced by kind permission of Friends of the Lake District.

CHAPTER EIGHT

The National Park campaign: 1940–1951

By the time of the Second World War, there was consensus across party lines that national land-use planning needed a much more effective bite than that afforded by the tentative and piecemeal legislation of the 1930s, a view shared by rural land-use experts like Dudley Stamp as by regional planners like Patrick Abercrombie. The vision for the future in England was set out by the reports of the Barlow Commission on the distribution of the industrial population in 1940, by that of the Scott Committee on planning in rural areas in 1942, by that of John Dower on National Park areas in 1945, and by that of the Hobhouse Committee on National Parks and Access in 1947. The main upshot for the countryside was the Town and Country Planning Act of 1947 that introduced the concept of a comprehensive system of development plans, and the National Parks and Countryside Act of 1949 that provided National Parks in England and Wales only, and a Nature Conservancy service in England, Wales and Scotland.

T. C. Smout, *Nature Contested*, p. 159.

This chapter examines the part played by FLD in the national park campaign, leading to the 1949 Act. The cross-connections of FLD officers with CPRE SCNP members have already been described (see Chapter Six). Here Birkett and Abercrombie played important roles. But the two key players are Symonds and Dower, the former taking an even higher profile after Dower's death in 1947. Thereafter Symonds (especially as drafting secretary of SCNP as well as secretary of FLD) took the leading role on the national stage in monitoring the passage of legislation, including the drafting of detailed amendments to the Bill, as it went through Parliament. The subsequent disappointments that FLD and CPRE experienced, particularly in the organisational and funding arrangements that were created as the Act was implemented, will be considered. And finally, the establishment of the boundaries of the new National Park and the setting up of the Lake District National Park Authority in 1951 are described.

The underlying assumptions shared by most local and national amenity groups, such as FLD, are pertinent. These assumptions radically coloured their thinking and the action that they wanted on the proposed legal framework for town and country planning and national parks. Two were of particular importance. One was the idea that the town and country planning system (which did not exist except on paper) would reconcile private land ownership and the exploitation of the natural resources of the parks with the public good, and thus ensure a harmonious, well-ordered, well-designed countryside. The other was that a prosperous farming industry would preserve both the rural landscape and the rural communities.[1] These assumptions run like a thread through the Scott, Dower and Hobhouse Reports.

Looking back on the post-war years with the benefit of hindsight, we now know, of course, that wholesale changes have taken place in the agricultural sector since 1945 and many of these changes – even in areas subsequently designated for national park status – have had a radical and detrimental effect on the nation's rural landscape, and consequently its flora and fauna. Therefore, it is easy for us to regard these assumptions as at best optimistic and at worst plain naïve. But these attitudes were coloured by the fact that there had been a general agricultural depression during the inter-war years. Policy thinking was that, by encouraging a healthy agricultural sector, the rural landscape would be preserved against undesirable developments without the need for strong planning and development controls. The key outcome was that the agricultural sector, including forestry, was largely excluded from the new post-war planning system. As a result 'although farming, forestry and woodland operations take up 96 per cent of the land surface of national parks, planning in the countryside is overwhelmingly concerned with the built development'.[2] This helps to explain why amenity groups such as FLD concentrated their policy objectives on responding to the potential adverse effects, as they saw them, of built developments in areas of natural beauty. Bluntly, in their view the main threat was from creeping urbanisation of the countryside, and assaults by public authorities and statutory bodies on the landscape and its natural resources.

During this period Symonds, Dower, Abercrombie and Birkett continued to work on behalf of FLD and CPRE SCNP. They met with ministers and civil servants (indeed, as we have seen, Dower himself was a 'temporary' civil servant within the Ministry of Works and Planning, changed later in the War to the Ministry of Town and Country Planning). The political climate was altering and the political landscape was to change dramatically with the election of a Labour government in 1945. The Scott Report of 1942, *Land utilisation in rural areas*, to which FLD and CPRE SCNP gave evidence, specifically reaffirmed the proposed establishment of national parks in England and Wales, to be delineated by a new Central Planning Commission. It was apposite that Birkett, as FLD president, was able make a rare attendance at FLD's

executive committee meeting on 27 August 1942, when the Scott Report
was discussed. He expressed his opinion that 'the general principle of
establishing national parks was won: all now depended upon the proper
execution of it, and that depended upon the formal adoption of the
principle by the government'. In September 1942, Symonds took over
from Dower as drafting secretary of CPRE SCNP. At FLD's executive
committee meeting on 24 September 1943, Symonds reported that he and
Birkett had been to see W. S. Morrison, the Minister of Town and
Country Planning, who had expressed his personal preference for
creating national parks and a National Parks Commission. Perhaps
naturally, he had not been specific about the Commission's organisation,
funding, duties and powers. Dower was now asked to write a follow-up
report on national parks, completed in 1943, and he had been in
correspondence with Symonds during the compilation of his internal
report. For example, he asked about the use of the proposed FLD
boundaries for a future national park area, and whether he should draw
up a more accurate map:

> Personally … I am sure that our old "pamphlet cover" boundary is too
> generous, especially by its inclusion of the whole of the Grange-
> Cartmel promontory … (I am clear that if they plant one at all, it
> must be an FLD boundary: there is no other body competent to
> propose one).

Symonds' pencilled note on Dower's letter retorted:

> Use own existing map as good enough. It would be a sheer waste of
> time to revise it now. Put a note that it is not intended to be an exact
> statement of detail at places where the boundary is clearly a matter of
> debate.[3]

Dower was then asked to reshape his internal report as a White Paper. The
Report on National Parks in England and Wales was published in April
1945. Dower and Symonds exchanged much correspondence between 1942
and 1945 on many national park matters (including the other potential
national parks) to inform the compilation of Dower's report.[4] As far as
Lake District boundaries were concerned, discussion included which areas
should be included or excluded, and they had to make value judgements
on what are now more formally known as landscape character assessments.
How much of the west coastline should be included? Dower suggested to
Symonds to 'concede the parishes of Seascale and Drigg to keep the rest of
the coast'.[5] St Bees Head was considered (Symonds favoured its inclusion)
but eventually omitted. On the north-eastern side, it was agreed to leave
out the Greystoke estates. The eastern border was not contentious, often
following the A6 (but excluding Shap and its quarries). Perhaps the most
debatable part of the boundary was in the Morecambe Bay area, and

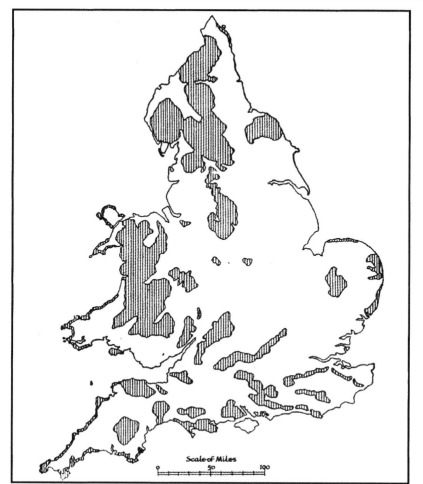

56 Dower's areas of search for national parks. From FLD archive, reproduced by kind permission of Friends of the Lake District.

especially the Cartmel-Grange peninsula. The FLD's boundary map, derived as it was from the early work of Abercrombie and Spence, included it. Dower favoured its virtual exclusion (the Hobhouse Committee subsequently compromised by limiting their recommended exclusions to Grange, Lindale and Meathop parish).[6]

The Labour Government elected in July 1945 was generally thought to be more committed to the national park ideal. For example, Lewis Silkin, the new minister of town and country planning, and Hugh Dalton, the chancellor of the exchequer, had personal associations with the ramblers' movement. Also, the Labour party was more in favour of the concept of national planning and the nationalisation of key industries and services. Expectations were high that the new government would be in favour not only of creating national parks but also setting up a central National Parks Commission with strong planning powers and the financial muscle to underpin and support them. This was not to be the case. The

57 Dower's recommended national parks. From FLD archive, reproduced by kind permission of Friends of the Lake District.

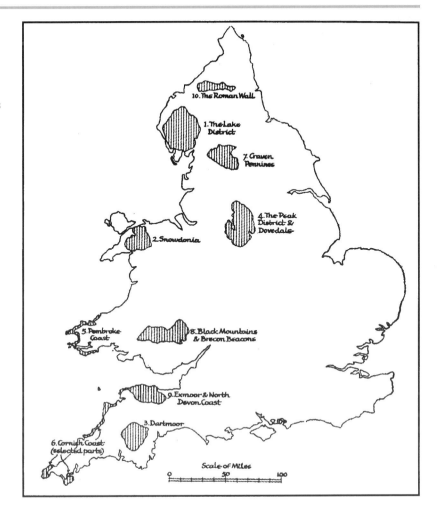

government came out in favour of national parks, but rejected the proposal for a strong National Parks Commission. Whether the cup was now half empty or half full depended on one's point of view. For FLD and other amenity groups it was half empty. For Symonds in particular it was more than half-empty.

The early signs were encouraging. The new government accepted Dower's report in principle. Dower tipped off Symonds that Silkin, the new minister, was going to set up a committee to make firm recommendations on the creation of specific national parks and their organisation, management and funding. Sir Arthur Hobhouse (CPRE executive committee member and chairman of Somerset County Council) was asked to convene and chair a National Parks Committee (England and Wales). FLD was well represented with three of the ten members, including Dower and Chorley (by then Lord Chorley of Kendal).[7] The subsequent *Report of the National Parks Committee (England and Wales)* was published in July 1947. Its general and detailed recommendations were mostly unsurprising since they were largely based on those for which both FLD and CPRE SCNP had been privately and publicly campaigning. Many were already in the Dower Report, itself substantially based on earlier work by FLD and CPRE SCNP. Hobhouse recommended 12 national parks for implementation in three tranches of four. The Lake District, together with North Wales, the Peak District and Dartmoor were in the first 'instalment'. But it was made clear that the 'order in which these [twelve] areas are arranged does not imply any attempted assessment of their relative beauty and recreational value, but takes account of geographical distribution and the need for protection'.[8]

The government's reaction to the Hobhouse Report should be seen in the wider context of the promised plans for wholescale review and reform of the town and country planning system at national and local level. The Town and Country Planning Act 1947 was the major element in the new arrangements. For the first time, local authorities were charged with preparing development plans for their areas. All new development and changes in land use would be subject to development controls, to ensure their conformity with these new development plans. In the rural areas, county councils were explicitly given these new powers and duties, so they were unlikely to want to cede these newly-gained planning roles to new – and as yet to be established – national park authorities to be set up in their areas. They therefore lobbied long and hard to retain their new planning functions at county level, not wanting to give any away to a central National Parks Commission, and also fought for local planning authorities in national park areas to be funded out of local rates, not national taxes.[9] In both these respects they had the crucial support of the government because of the political implications at central government level of taking Hobhouse fully on board. Furthermore government departments and public authorities remained largely exempt from the new planning regime. No departmental minister or public authority chairman would freely allow a new and powerful National Parks Commission to have the final say or veto on whether proposed developments should go ahead or not in the new national park areas. But for Symonds 'The protection of national parks against Government departments – in other words the status of the Commission when it is in conflict with these departments – is obviously the crucial point in the whole Bill'.[10]

The die was cast soon after the Hobhouse Report was published in July 1947. On 3 December 1947 a deputation from CPRE (including Symonds and Griffin) met with the Minister of Town and Country Planning (Silkin) and his senior staff. At this meeting Silkin revealed his, and therefore the government's, thinking. It was made clear that having 'created new and larger Planning Authorities under the 1947 Town and

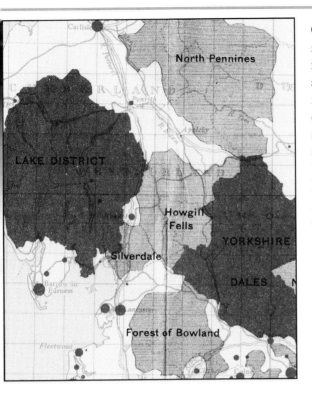

58 Hobhouse national park boundaries. From FLD archive, reproduced by kind permission of Friends of the Lake District.

Country Planning Act he would be reluctant to take planning powers away from them before they had a chance to show what they could do'. CPRE replied that since they saw government departments and public agencies, such as the Forestry Commission and water and electricity utilities, as the main 'menace' there needed to be a strong National Parks Commission, with a robust planning framework, reporting directly to Minister for Town and Country Planning. Silkin disagreed: he thought that the 1947 Act 'could adequately safeguard the National Park areas through the new larger [local] Planning Authorities'. Therefore, he saw the role of the National Parks Commission as purely an advisory one 'so far as planning was concerned'. Lastly, to emphasise the point, he said that a National Parks Commission having its own statutory planning role 'would mean telling some 20 out of the 63 County Councils that we could not trust them to do the job and the powers must be handed over to a non-elected body'.[11]

In spite of intense work behind the scenes by CPRE, FLD and other local, regional and national amenity groups, nothing changed fundamentally between 1947 and 1949 to shift government thinking on the organisational aspects of national parks. It has been alleged that 'Ministers attempted to conceal the gulf that separated the 1949 Act from the Dower and Hobhouse reports by claiming that 90% of their recommendations had been accepted'. Furthermore, 'Inside the Civil Service the National Parks Commission (to Symonds a non-commission) was seen as an unnecessary body the only real function of which was to provide a sop to the national parks lobby'.[12]

The National Parks and Access to the Countryside Act was passed on 16 December 1949. Its main provisions can be summarised under the headings of national park designation and purposes, national park organisation, management arrangements and funding, nature and landscape conservation arrangements and functions, and the right to roam. Part 2 of the Act defined areas to be designated as:

those extensive tracts of country which … by reason of a) their natural beauty, and b) the opportunities they afford for open air recreation having regard to their character and to their position in relation to centres of population, it is especially desirable that the necessary measures shall be taken for the purposes mentioned in the last foregoing subsection.

This meant that the two purposes of 'natural beauty' and 'recreation access' were directly linked to designation, principles which have scarcely changed over the years.[13] Clearly the Lake District qualified as a national park on that basis.

Organisation and funding

At national level a National Parks Commission (NPC) was established. However, its only statutory purpose was to consider as appropriate the designation and setting up of national parks, including their boundaries, and make recommendations to the Minister of Local Government and Planning. It had no other executive, administrative, landowning or land managing functions. Its role was entirely advisory and supervisory. The Commission was to have no full-time members: only its chairman and vice chairman were paid, and it had no specialist or local staff or role. Harold Abrahams, in charge of staff, was an Olympic athlete, whose main hobbies were said to be sports journalism and broadcasting.

At local level, many county councils continued to object to autonomous national park authorities. However, Cumberland, Westmorland and Lancashire County Councils now dropped their objections in principle to the creation of a Lake District National Park Authority. But they lobbied long and hard for the new national park authority to be created and run on their terms. Hugh Dalton (Minister of Town and Country Planning in 1949) agreed with their proposals. Thus the new Lake District National Park Authority (LDNPA) would be administered by a joint planning board, with no chief officer or planning staff of its own. It would be staffed by the three county council's existing planning officers, thus remaining essentially a sub-committee of the three county councils. Staff would be deemed to be working 'jointly' when they met to discuss national parks. In addition each of the three local authorities wanted to continue to have its part of the Lake District included in their own separate county development plans. As for LDNPA funding, it was to be from local rates not central taxation. CPRE's SCNP and FLD continued to lobby hard against all these proposals after the Act was passed. However, they were swimming against a very strong tide at both central and local government level. In the end all they achieved was the setting up of a new LDNPA that was to be administered as a single joint planning board (not a multi-county council committee). It would therefore be responsible for formulating its own development plan, and act as the planning authority for its own area. However, on the crucial matter of funding the government agreed with the three county councils to cap its initial annual expenditure at £7,500. A crumb of comfort was tossed to CPRE and FLD: when the LDNPA was finally established, it was agreed to review these administrative arrangements after three years.

Landscape and conservation arrangements and responsibilities

The Hobhouse Report had recognised that there would be potential for overlap and conflict between the new national parks and any new national nature and wildlife conservation body. It therefore recommended that 'the proposed National Parks Commission must have full responsibility for the conservation of nature in national parks, and this must form an integral part of their policy and day-to-day management'.[14] This did not happen. Nature conservation became the responsibility of the new Nature Conservancy. This was a largely scientific, research-based body, with its own management structure and resources. It was to recommend areas to be designated as national nature reserves and sites of special scientific interest (SSSIs), and its research-based interests were to be secured through the setting up of the Institute of Terrestrial Ecology and Freshwater Biological Association. Both bodies had their headquarters in or near the new Lake District National Park, the former near Grange-over-Sands and the latter beside Windermere, opposite Bowness. Since the definition of 'natural beauty' was taken to include flora and fauna, there was the potential for overlap and conflict that Hobhouse had sought to avoid.

The right to roam

As far as access to the countryside or the 'right to roam', as it has become known, was concerned, Part V of the 1949 Act 'stood the principles of the Scott, Dower and Hobhouse reports on their heads'.[15] The public were to have no rights of access except by landowners' agreement. It was not until the Countryside and Rights of Way Act of 2000 that this wrong – as FLD and other amenity groups saw it – was righted. However, Part IV of the Act did allow for the creation of new statutory public rights of way. This stopped the piecemeal loss that had taken place during the 1930s and 1940s. Further, the new LDNPA, and not the county councils as elsewhere, was to be given the duty to carry out a survey of all existing rights of way and prepare and maintain definitive rights of way maps for the Lake District. It was also given the new statutory right to create, divert or close rights of way. FLD warmly welcomed this part of the Act for which it had long lobbied. It was well prepared for this outcome, and as we have seen had already begun to carry out its own survey of rights of way during the 1930s and 1940s. And it would continue to rely on FLD people such as Symonds and Philip Cleave (the first full-time FLD secretary), with their detailed knowledge of the area and energy and tenacity, to make the necessary representations to get up-to-date and accurate surveys and maps published.

Although the National Parks and Access to the Countryside Act was passed on 16 December 1949 it took time before any new national parks (and Areas of Outstanding Natural Beauty) could be recommended, accepted and created. First, the National Parks Commission (NPC) had to be set up, located and staffed. Its first chairman was Sir Patrick Duff. The NPC needed to examine the Hobhouse recommendations, including suitable areas for consideration, and agree or reject them. Next they had to examine, recommend and consult on the boundaries of proposed parks, and make recommendations for the Minister of Local Government and Planning to accept or reject. All this would take time. In fact, as Hobhouse had recommended in 1947, the Lake District, the Peak District, Snowdonia and Dartmoor were in the first tranche, to be given priority for consideration and designation. The Peak District National Park was designated on 17 April 1951; the Lake District National Park designation followed shortly after on 9 May 1951.[16] After designation, the new planning authority had to be set up, and its administration and funding agreed. Throughout this period lobbying continued at national level (with CPRE SCNP) about the proposed structure and organisation and funding of the new LDNPA.

The first informal meeting in the Lake District between FLD and NPC staff took place in June 1950. In carrying out its survey on the ground NPC was happy to follow the Hobhouse boundary recommendations. It was also very receptive to current FLD views. As already outlined (in Chapter Six), FLD had already prepared the position during the 1930s and 1940s and the Hobhouse proposals were largely the FLD proposals anyway. FLD now offered its thinking on the fine-tuning of the proposed boundary as follows. Firstly, parish boundaries should be used where possible, and not roads. Secondly, the west coast from the north of Drigg parish to the southern part of Whicham parish should be included. Thirdly, some parishes along the lower Derwent in the north should be excluded. Finally, in the south some ten parishes in the Furness and Cartmel areas should be excluded.[17] Subject to further fine-tuning, these proposed boundaries to the future national park were agreed by NPC.[18] The exact line of the boundaries was decided by a group, mainly made up of members of the NPC. They stayed in the Lake District and toured the perimeter by coach, examining the route on the ground 'by beck, hedge and, mainly minor, roads where parishes were divided, as the Hobhouse Committee had done before'.[19]

Thus FLD can take the major credit for suggesting and securing these boundaries. It could also take some credit for the fact that:

> The Secretary of NPC had received confirmation from the Minister of Local Government and Planning that the constitution of a Joint Planning Board will necessitate a fresh development plan for the national park area. Schemes approved in the previous development plan would not be binding on the Joint Planning Board.[20]

However, FLD success in this was not mirrored when it came to the proposed organisation and funding of the new LDNPA. After designation in May 1951, the three county councils continued to lobby hard with the government. A deputation was sent to the new Minister of Local Government and Planning, Harold Macmillan. He subsequently agreed to their suggestion that when creating the new LDNPA he would give it complete discretion on how it ran its own internal organisation and administration. Further he also confirmed the cap on the initial annual budget of £7,500, to be shared equally by each local authority from local rates. The new Lake District Planning Board was to have 18 representatives. Each county council should have four members, with the addition of six 'national' members. The financial cap meant that the shape of national park authority organisation and staffing was fixed from the start: there could be no chief officer and no independent planning staff. It is clear that FLD in general, and Symonds in particular, took this badly. However, when both Symonds and Philip Cleave were invited by the NPC to accept nomination as 'national' members of the LDNPA they were wise and realistic enough to consent 'though without eagerness'.[21] It was realised that it was more useful to try to make the new arrangements work from the inside, as well as lobbying for structural change from the sidelines.

The first meeting of the LDNPA took place in Kendal on 24 September 1951. The worth of having the FLD voice heard within the new organisation was soon shown. When it came to suggestions for inclusions in the Planning Board's first annual programme, Symonds and Cleave put forward three ideas: first, to suggest a schedule of 'green roads' (such as the Garburn Pass), for possible traffic restriction orders; second, to carry out a survey of rural 'cottages' of vernacular architectural interest; and third, the assumption of powers under the 1949 Act to create new public footpaths, with two specific proposals for new footpaths along the western shore of Windermere. These were subsequently included in the first LDNPA annual programme with three others, a survey of rural industries, a review of car parking spaces and the identification and removal of unsightly temporary buildings and mine refuse.

During the 1950s CPRE SCNP and FLD continued to lobby and campaign for a review of national park administration – without success.

In those early years it was a case of making do and working with what was there. It has been well said that the new LDNPA was:

> an educator, a controller of building, and, increasingly, a diplomat dealing with a multitude of official and private agencies. [Further] the early Annual Reports suggest the role of a very well-meaning Canute standing firmly before a flood of water and electricity schemes put forward by statutory and other authorities, and facing continual problems posed by equally powerful public transport bodies ... which liked traffic but which were not interested in the remoter farming communities which the Planning Board had under its moral wing ... Non-elected, but consisting of highly responsible appointees, the Board seemed to resemble one of the remote statutory bodies which created many of its own problems.[22]

So can the FLD/CPRE national park campaign during the 1930s and 1940s be judged as successful? It could be argued that, looking back from today's perspective, we might come to a different conclusion to those holding the tiller at the time. After all, one of the main objects of FLD upon its formation in 1934 was the setting up of national parks in general and for the Lake District in particular. The establishment of national parks was enshrined in legislation in 1949, and, as has been demonstrated, a major credit for this success is due to FLD and CPRE – and especially a few key people representing both FLD and CPRE. Therefore, one might fairly say that the overall objective was achieved. But it is clear that this is not how it was seen at the time. The national park principle was accepted, but the organisational and funding arrangements to go with their establishment were best seen as a 'milk and water' affair. In particular, there was no strong National Parks Commission with the power to override other government departments, public bodies/utilities and local authorities; and no Lake District unitary planning authority with its own professional staff to act as a local national park champion. In the view FLD and other amenity groups national park areas were therefore still left exposed and vulnerable to undesirable landscape change. The sense of 'unfinished business' is reflected in the revised objects of FLD agreed at the 1948 AGM. They were now much simplified to reflect the new circumstances:

> To promote an energetic and consistent application of a unified planning policy for the Lake District as a whole, under effective statutory powers created by legislation for National Parks; to organize concerted action for protecting the landscape and natural beauty of the Lake District; and to co-operate with and support other bodies having similar objects and interests.

It is not possible to write a story of the campaign for national parks or FLD's early years without taking into account the role that Reverend H. H. Symonds played. Certainly his contemporaries who knew and worked with him were convinced of his importance and said so too. Thus Herbert Griffin (CPRE secretary) wrote a letter on 22 February 1950 to all members of SCNP:

59 Reverend H. H. Symonds in his later years. From FLD archive, reproduced by kind permission of Friends of the Lake District.

"Symonds Luncheon"

You will remember that at the last meeting of the Standing Committee the question of paying some tribute to Symonds for the tremendous amount of work which he put in on our behalf in connection with the National Parks Bill was raised and it was decided to arrange a luncheon, at which Sir Norman Birkett would preside.

At short notice, 25 people came to the event held in Symond's honour at the Prince Consort Room of the Albert Hall, London on 18 March 1950. At the same time a press release was put out in Birkett's name as Chairman of CPRE SCNP:

A complimentary luncheon was given on Saturday, March 18th, to the Rev. H.H. Symonds, the Hon. Drafting Secretary to the Standing Committee on National Parks, in acknowledgement of his long and devoted service to the Committee and to the cause of National Parks.

While the late Mr. John Dower was alive, Mr. Symonds worked in close co-operation with him in this connection and by his publications and memoranda on various aspects of the problem, helped the Standing Committee to keep the matter before the public in such a way as to ensure that when proposals for the establishment of National Parks were at long last embodied in a Parliamentary Bill, Parliament and the Minister in charge were left in no doubt as to the strength of public support the measure commanded.

Sir Norman Birkett, the Chairman of the Standing Committee, who presided, said:

> "The passing of the National Parks Act seemed to us a suitable occasion when we could pay tribute to the immense services of Mr. Symonds. For many years he has fought a most valiant fight for the establishment of National Parks, and to that fight he brought not only detailed and exact knowledge, but an industry and devotion of the most striking kind. It would be ungracious not to acknowledge the great step forward taken by the Government which has resulted in the passing of the Act. Despite the urgency of the matter, and the pressure of public opinion, previous governments have been content to do nothing. The Standing Committee is therefore most grateful to the Government for recognising officially that National Parks are public possessions of the most valuable kind. At the same time, it was impossible not to feel a strong sense of disappointment that the Act fell short in some respects of what the Standing Committee has fought for during the past twelve years. It was to be hoped that the shortcomings would be remedied in the near future, and the Committee would continue its work to this end. In particular, the Committee would work for more effective control by the National Parks Commission, so that the dangers to National Parks, which were very real, might be overcome."

To this end the Standing Committee on National Parks of the Council for the Protection of Rural England and the Council for the Protection of Rural Wales have pledged themselves to do everything in their power to help the National Parks Commission to make the best possible use of the Act.

However, in commenting on the draft press release to Griffin, Birkett 'made a telling comment', in a handwritten postscript: 'I doubt whether Symonds would unbend enough to say "Thank you" to the Government at all! But I think we should, and then go on to suggest strengthening'.[23]

Notes

[1] See A. & M. MacEwen, *National Parks: conservation or cosmetics?* (London: G. Allen & Unwin, 1982), p. 9.

[2] Ibid, p. 11. Hobhouse did go so far as to recommend that planning controls be extended to include new farm buildings within the agricultural sector. Changes in agricultural land use and land design and layout were, however, to be left to the market 'It would be wrong to oppose an evolution in farming practice which would bring added national prosperity. If, however, conversion from heather moor to grassland were undertaken on a large scale it might be necessary for the National Parks Commission to acquire and preserve limited areas of moorland for the sake of their natural beauty or interest'. Hobhouse Report. Paragraph 123, p. 29.

3   CRO (Kendal) WDSO 117/b6/107 – letter Dower to Symonds 20 October 1942.

4   See S. M. Clark, 'Perceptions of the boundaries of the Lake District from 18th century, to the designation of the National Park' Unpublished Diploma Dissertation, University of Lancaster, 1994.

5   Clark, p. 37.

6   See Clark, pp. 35–41.

7   The Committee had two offshoots. A Special Committee on Footpaths and Access to the Countryside, chaired by Hobhouse, and the Wildlife Special Conservation Committee, chaired by Sir Julian Huxley. All three reported in 1947.

8   The other recommended national parks were the Yorkshire Dales, the Pembrokeshire Coast, Exmoor, and the South Downs (Second Instalment); and The Roman Wall, the North York Moors, Brecon Beacons and Black Mountains, and the Broads (Third Instalment). Hobhouse, paragraph 36, p. 10.

9   Furthermore, the county councils objected to the designation of all the national parks, except Northumberland and Dartmoor.

10   FLD *Annual Report and Newsletter*, 1949, p. 3.

11   CPRE C/1/102/40 (ex 232/26).

12   MacEwen, p. 18.

13   It is clear that purposes a) and b) could be in conflict on some occasions (for example, 4 x 4 vehicles and motor cycles on the fells). It was not until the Sandford Report (1976) that it became policy that where access and protection of the natural beauty were in conflict the latter should take precedence over the former.

14   Hobhouse Report paragraph 274, p. 61.

15   MacEwen, p. 19.

16   The other six were designated as follows: Pembrokeshire Coast (1952), North York Moors (1952), Yorkshire Dales (1954), Exmoor (1954), Northumberland (including the Roman Wall) (1956), and Brecon Beacons (1957). Nine were in Dowers's first instalment (he excluded North York Moors, but included the Cornish coast). Hobhouse also included the Broads which became a de facto National Park in 1989; New Forest became one in 2005; South Downs was created in 2009.

17   FLD Minutes 2 September 1950. Most of these had been discussed between John Dower and Hal Symonds during the early 1940s.

18   FLD Minutes 2 December 1950.

19   Clark, p. 41.

20   FLD Minutes 2 June 1950.

21   FLD Minutes 11 August 1951.

22   Marshall and Walton, pp. 230–231.

23   CPRE SR C/1/102/43.

60 Wastwater. From FLD archive, reproduced by kind permission of Friends of the Lake District.

CHAPTER NINE

Afterword – battles and beauty

The increasing acceptability of environmental arguments over the course of the twentieth century has allowed the amenity societies to shame and rebuke potential developers who have transgressed the codes of conduct set for the Lake District by the preservationist interest. In dispute after dispute, it is possible to see the party of development, so to speak, having to come to terms with the enduring images of beauty and fragility associated with the area.

C. O'Neill and J. K. Walton in D. W. G. Hind and J. P. Mitchell (eds.), *Sustainable Tourism in the English Lake District*, 2004, p. 42.

How should FLD be judged on the record of its early years? There is sufficient evidence to express the view that in a very short time it had established itself at both local and national levels as a credible, important and influential landscape conservation group. It was increasingly listened to, and its views deemed important, based as they were on thoroughly professional and informed analysis, even if others did not always agree with them. Moreover, its views on the special qualities that can be attributed to specific rural landscapes, and the concomitant need to protect them from 'undesirable' developments (if within a 'narrow' regional focus), increasingly struck a chord within the developing broader landscape conservation movement throughout the country. However, like other regional landscape amenity groups, it had to adapt to a world in which the influence of local authorities and local landowners on changes to the regional landscape was increasingly extended to other groups by various national government, public authority and public utility proposals and developments (for example, large-scale afforestation, the creation of a national electricity grid and the military occupation and use of land).

This was especially challenging for FLD, because, although it had a national membership, it plainly had a regional focus. Using influence at regional and local level to inform local proposals for landscape change deemed 'inappropriate' was one thing, getting its voice heard at national level was quite another challenge, particularly when decisions were being taken remotely and centrally. However, even the nationally-based amenity organisations such as CPRE, the National Trust, Youth Hostels

Association, Ramblers' Association and Commons, Open Spaces and Footpaths Society could also struggle to get their views heard and accepted. But it was also true that although FLD shared a common landscape conservation rationale with many of these organisations, especially CPRE and the National Trust, they sometimes disagreed with each other. But, importantly, when they did disagree it was usually about tactics, not ends. The starkest example of this difference is probably exhibited in the 'afforestation quarrel' described in Chapter Three. As we have also seen, the same people serviced many of these amenity groups at the top, notably Symonds, Spence, Dower, Chorley, Abercrombie and Birkett, all of whom were active at one time or another in many and/or all of these organisations.

Certainly FLD has often been pictured, with some justification (at the time and in hindsight), as being more radical in its lobbying and campaigning approach to conservation issues than the other local and national amenity groups. And like any other group, it had its share of successes and failures, as it recognised itself at the time. Moreover, it was not necessarily always representative of majority public opinion in opposing some development proposals as 'undesirable' in principle and/or detail, insofar as any wide consensus existed at the time. For example, a significant number of local residents in the Windermere area were undoubtedly in favour of retaining the 'temporary housing' estate at Calgarth Park and its nearby aircraft factory site. Furthermore, it would be interesting to know how the public, whether at local and national level, felt about the value of creating national parks during the 1930s and 1940s, let alone on issues such as their boundaries and organisational and funding arrangements. This is not surprising. As stressed in the introduction, arguments for or against landscape protection and conservation inevitably involve value judgements and trade-offs. Beauty is in the eye of the beholder and opinions will always differ.

However, it is important to emphasise that before the Lake District National Park was established in 1951 there was no formal single 'champion' charged with securing the protection of the Lake District as a whole as the area fell within Lancashire, Westmorland and Cumberland county council boundaries. It was this vacuum that FLD filled. And I think the evidence is there to adjudge FLD as very important and influential in acting as a major advocate and 'spear-carrier', alongside CPRE, for the Lake District's 'special qualities' as increasingly articulated and defined during the 1930s and 1940s. It was these 'special qualities' which informed the reaction of FLD and other amenity groups to local development proposals. And it was also these 'special qualities' that determined and justified its selection, together with other 'special' parts of England and Wales, for national park status from 1951. Thus, for all the disappointments expressed by amenity groups for the 'missed

51 Clouds over
Bowfell. From FLD
archive, reproduced
by kind permission
of Friends of the
Lake District.

opportunities' and 'inherent weaknesses' of the 1949 National Parks and
Access to the Countryside Act, it can be said that the long campaign to
get them set up was successful.

With this major milestone achieved, and once the Lake District
National Park Authority was established in 1951 as the 'statutory guardian
of the Lake District', the whole agenda and debate changed. The
campaign for national parks was won. The campaign to strengthen their
powers and duties now began and would continue over the following
decades. This would start a whole new phase in the development of the
national park movement. It would also start a new phase in the FLD
story, in its new role as a 'critical friend' of the Lake District National
Park Authority.

Bibliography

Primary sources

1.   <u>Records of Friends of the Lake District (FLD)</u>
1.1 *FLD office, Murley Moss, Kendal*
       Books of Minutes FLD Executive Committee Meetings: 1934–1948; 1948–1952.
       Book of Minutes of FLD Annual General Meetings: 1934–1960.
       FLD Annual Reports and Newsletters: 1934–1952.
1.2 *Cumbria Record Office, Kendal*
       Friends of the Lake District Collection: CRO WDSO/117.
       CRO WDSO/B/117/VI/1 & 2. Afforestation: the early years up to the 1936 White Paper.
       CRO WDSO/117/B/VI/10. Electricity: Borrowdale electricity scheme.
       CRO WDSO/117/B/VI/32 & 33. Calgarth Housing Estate.
       CRO WDSO/117/B/VI/68 & 107. Dower/Symonds Correspondence.
       CRO WDSO/117/B/VI/105/1. Lake District Farm Estates.
       CRO WDSO/117/C/III/1. Collection of c100 mounted photographs for use in pre-[Second World] war exhibitions: indexed. (Digitised – 2009).
       Rawnsley Papers: CRO WDSO/422/2.
       CRO WDSO/422/2/7. English Lake District Association Report and Accounts, 1922.
       CRO WDSO/422/2/8. Spence letter to Mrs Rawnsley.
       Fell & Rock Climbing Club Collection: CRO WDSO/163.
       CRO WDSO/163/Record Box Two. Minutes of Meetings 1907–1947.

2.   <u>Records of the Council for the Preservation of Rural England (CPRE)</u> now the Campaign to Protect Rural England (CPRE)
2.1 *CPRE head office library, London*
       Monthly Reports: 1927–1951.
       Annual Reports: 1927–1951.
2.2 *Museum of Rural Life, University of Reading, Reading*
       CPRE Collection: SR CPRE.

SR CPRE C/1/36/4–7. Calgarth seaplane factory and estate 1940–1966.

SR CPRE C/89/28–34. Lake District Afforestation 1935–1938.

SR CPRE C/102/1–3. National Parks 1929–1936.

SR CPRE C/102/10–14. National Parks 1936–1939.

SR CPRE C/102/16. Lake District National Committee Resolution and Three Counties Conference 1931.

SR CPRE C/102/19. Lake District Regional Plan 1935.

SR CPRE C/102/20. Friends of the Lake District 1934–1937.

SR CPRE C/102/40 & 41. John Dower and Hobhouse Reports on National Parks in England & Wales 1945–1948 & 1948–1950.

SR CPRE C/102/43. Reverend Henry Herbert Symonds 1945–1979.

SR CPRE C/102/52. National Park Boundaries 1950–1951.

Westmorland Gazette newspaper archive on microfiche at Cumbria Local Studies Library, Kendal.

Secondary sources

P. Abercrombie, *The Preservation of Rural England – The Control of Development by means of Rural Planning* (London: Hodder & Stoughton, 1926).

P. Abercrombie and S. A. Kelly, *Cumbrian Regional Planning Scheme* (London: Hodder & Stoughton Ltd., 1932).

C. Addison, *Report of the National Park Committee* (London: Cmnd 3851, HMSO, 1931).

Afforestation in the Lake District – A Report by the Joint Informal Committee of the Forestry Commission and the Council for the Preservation of Rural England (London: HMSO, 1936).

E. Battrick, *Guardian of the Lakes: a history of the National Trust in the Lake District from 1946* (Kendal: Westmorland Gazette, 1987).

G. Berry and G. Beard, *The Lake District: a Century of Conservation* (Edinburgh: John Bartholomew, 1980).

I. Brodie, *Forestry in the Lake District* (Kendal: Friends of the Lake District, 2004).

S. M. Clark, 'Perceptions of the boundaries of the Lake District from 18th century, to the designation of the National Park', unpublished Diplona dissertation, University of Lancaster, 1994.

J. H. Cousins, 'Lake District Farm Estates Ltd., a History: 1937–1977', unpublished Diploma dissertation, University of Lancaster, 2000 (Copy also held at FLD Office, Kendal).

J. Dower, *National Parks in England and Wales* (London: Cmnd 6378 HMSO, 1945).

R. Ellis, 'The Keswick trespasses: working class protest or gentleman's agreement?' unpublished Diploma dissertation, Lancaster University, 2008.

Sir J. J. Harwood. *History and Description of the Thirlmere Water Scheme* (Manchester, Henry Blackwood & Co., 1895).

P. Hindle, *Roads and Tracks of the Lake District* (Milnthorpe: Cicerone Press, 1998).

D. W. G Hind & J. P. Mitchell (eds.), *Sustainable Tourism in the English Lake District* (Sunderland: Business Education Publishers Ltd., 2004).

Sir A. Hobhouse (Chairman), *Report of the National Parks Committee (England and Wales)*, London: Cmnd 7121 (HMSO, 1947).

Allan King, *Wings on Windermere: the history of the Lake District's forgotten flying boat factory* (Poland: Stratus, 2009).

Lake District National Park Authority, *Lake District National Management Plan* (Kendal: LDNPA, 2004).

A. & M. MacEwen, *National Parks: conservation or cosmetics?* (London: G. Allen and Unwin, 1982).

A. & M. MacEwen, *Greenprints for the Countryside? The Story of Britain's National Parks* (London: G. Allen & Unwin, 1987).

J. D. Marshall and J. K. Walton, *The Lake Counties from 1830 to the mid-twentieth century* (Manchester: Manchester University Press, 1981).

R. H. Mattocks, *The Lake District (South) Regional Planning Scheme* (Kendal: Atkinson and Pollitt, 1930).

L. M. Mullet, '"The blast of a foghorn during the performance of a Brahm's symphony": afforestation in the Lake District and its role in the Friends of the Lake District conservation movement in the 1930s', unpublished Diploma dissertation, Lancaster University, 2007.

G. Murphy, *Founders of the National Trust* (London: Christopher Helm, 1987).

N. Nicholson, *The Lakers* (Milnthorpe: Cicerone Press, 1995 edition).

N. Nicholson, *The Lake District, An Anthology* (Harmondsworth: Middlesex: Penguin Books, 1978).

W. Rollinson (ed.), *The Lake District Landscape Heritage* (Newton Abbott: David & Charles, 1989).

F. R. Sandbach, 'The early campaign for a National Park in the Lake District', *I.B.G. Transactions and Papers*, Vol. 3, no. 4, 1978, pp. 498–513.

Mr Justice Scott (Chairman), *Report of the Committee on land utilisation in rural areas* (London: Cmnd 6378 HMSO, 1942).

T. C. Smout, *Nature Contested: Environmental History in Scotland and Northern England since 1600* (Edinburgh: Edinburgh University Press, 2000).

H. H. Symonds, *Afforestation in the Lake District* (London: J. M. Dent and Sons Ltd., 1936).

H. H. Symonds, *Walking in the Lake District* (London: A. Maclehose & Co., 1933).

B. L. Thompson, *The Lake District and the National Trust* (Kendal: Titus Wilson, 1946).

C. E. Williams (ed.), *Britain and the Beast* (London: J. M. Dent and Sons Ltd., 1937).

A J. L Winchester & A. G. Crosby, *England's Landscape – The North West: English Heritage, Volume 8* (London: Collins, 2006).

W. Wordsworth (ed. de Selincourt), *Guide to the Lakes* (Oxford: Oxford University Press, 1977).

www.flyingboatsonline.org – Second World War: Calgarth seaplane factory and housing accommodation website.

Appendix 1

FLD OFFICEHOLDERS: 1934–1951

President
1934–1939	Lord Howarth of Penrith
1939–1957	Norman Birkett (Sir, 1941; Lord, 1958)

Vice President
1934–1946	Archbishop of York (William Temple)
1946–1960	Lord Chorley

Chairman
1934–1937	James W. Cropper
1937–1948	Canon F. T. Wilcox
1948–1955	Rev. H. H. Symonds

Treasurer
1934–1937	Mrs J. K. Spence
1937–1948	Alan Hargreaves
1949–1964	Graham Watson

Hon. Legal Adviser
1934–1936	W. F. Ascroft
1937–1956	J. Hopkinson

Hon. Secretary
1934–1937	Kenneth Spence
1937–1948	Rev. H. H. Symonds

Secretary
1947–1966	Philip Cleave

Hon Technical Adviser/Planning Consultant
1934–1938	Patrick Abercrombie
1939–1943	John Dower
1944+	lapsed

Appendix 2

Text of a handwritten draft letter from James Cropper (FLD Chairman) to Sir Francis Acland, a member of the Forestry Commission.

The letter was never sent. It was written end May/beginning of June 1935

Dear Francis,

I am being forced by the strongest local opinion to take part in the opposition to your planting schemes in Eskdale. I gather that you are in the thick of it on the other side. (I see that you were present at a meeting with delegates from the CPRE on April 30th)

The local people are not quite happy about the way the CPRE seem to be handling the situation. We sent them a very strong report, asking them to oppose the project – But as far as we can make out they have pushed aside our report and have taken it upon themselves the position of arbitrator between the out & out opponents & the Forestry Commission & are expecting that we shall be prepared to accept the very meagre compromise that the FC is putting forward. (We have never put our case into their hands. But we gather that (Sir Roy Robinson hopes to find) you are finding them more amenable than the Friends of the Lake District and hope to be able to conclude a pact with the CPRE & the National Trust that will be binding on us) I think it only fair to point out that we have not agreed to (this in any way) put our case in their hands – & that as far as I can judge the temper of (local) Lake District opinion – the opposition will be as wholehearted & active as ever whatever any outside bodies may agree to put up with,

We now have a (further) report of a further meeting on May 28th. Great stress is laid on a new factor (brought out in the report that we have received of that meeting). The Forestry Commission seem to consider themselves bound to plant because of some promise they have made when they acquired the property. It is difficult to see how such a promise can be binding if the planting can be shown to be detrimental to (the beauty of the countryside) the Lake District.

We have offered to take over the property at a reasonable profit to the Forestry Commission – We are met with a proposal that the public should pay £2 an acre for what is saved from (destruction) disfigurement & not have the freehold after that. Knowing what was paid for the property such a proposal strikes us as dangerously like blackmail.

It does seem a tragedy that the Forestry Commission cannot say that they find there is strong opposition to any further planting in the Lake Country & that they will transfer their activities elsewhere. We know they are a powerful body – & can override all & any (opposition if they are determined to do so) opponents however ? they may be. But if they plant (in the face of strong local opposition) with a stiff neck they must realize that young plantations are (very) peculiarly vulnerable in a large mountainous country & that it may be expensive to safeguard them to a profitable maturity.

I think (we have) the Lake District has a very good case (But they would not gain any public support if they did) and the Commissioners would be risking the loss of much public support (if they did do) if they push through their projects in the face of public opinion – The public do have some say in the voting of their funds.

(Copy of this draft letter provided to the author by Cropper's grandson J. A. Cropper.)

Index